This planner belongs to:

Twenty-two

January

S	M	T	W	T	F	S
						1
2	3	4	5	6	7	8
9	10	11	12	13	14	15
16	17	18	19	20	21	22
23	24	25	26	27	28	29
30	31					

February

S	M	T	W	T	F	S
		1	2	3	4	5
6	7	8	9	10	11	12
13	14	15	16	17	18	19
20	21	22	23	24	25	26
27	28					

March

S	M	T	W	T	F	S
		1	2	3	4	5
6	7	8	9	10	11	12
13	14	15	16	17	18	19
20	21	22	23	24	25	26
27	28	29	30	31		

April

S	M	T	W	T	F	S
					1	2
3	4	5	6	7	8	9
10	11	12	13	14	15	16
17	18	19	20	21	22	23
24	25	26	27	28	29	30

May

S	M	T	W	T	F	S
1	2	3	4	5	6	7
8	9	10	11	12	13	14
15	16	17	18	19	20	21
22	23	24	25	26	27	28
29	30	31				

June

S	M	T	W	T	F	S
			1	2	3	4
5	6	7	8	9	10	11
12	13	14	15	16	17	18
19	20	21	22	23	24	25
26	27	28	29	30		

July

S	M	T	W	T	F	S
					1	2
3	4	5	6	7	8	9
10	11	12	13	14	15	16
17	18	19	20	21	22	23
24	25	26	27	28	29	30
31						

August

S	M	T	W	T	F	S
	1	2	3	4	5	6
7	8	9	10	11	12	13
14	15	16	17	18	19	20
21	22	23	24	25	26	27
28	29	30	31			

September

S	M	T	W	T	F	S
				1	2	3
4	5	6	7	8	9	10
11	12	13	14	15	16	17
18	19	20	21	22	23	24
25	26	27	28	29	30	

October

S	M	T	W	T	F	S
						1
2	3	4	5	6	7	8
9	10	11	12	13	14	15
16	17	18	19	20	21	22
23	24	25	26	27	28	29
30	31					

November

S	M	T	W	T	F	S
		1	2	3	4	5
6	7	8	9	10	11	12
13	14	15	16	17	18	19
20	21	22	23	24	25	26
27	28	29	30			

December

S	M	T	W	T	F	S
				1	2	3
4	5	6	7	8	9	10
11	12	13	14	15	16	17
18	19	20	21	22	23	24
25	26	27	28	29	30	31

Year in Pixels

	J	F	M	A	M	J	J	A	S	O	N	D
1.												
2.												
3.												
4.												
5.												
6.												
7.												
8.												
9.												
10.												
11.												
12.												
13.												
14.												
15.												
16.												
17.												
18.												
19.												
20.												
21.												
22.												
23.												
24.												
25.												
26.												
27.												
28.												
29.												
30.												
31.												

Color Codes

Notes

January 2022

MONDAY	TUESDAY	WEDNESDAY	THURSDAY
3	4	5	6
10	11	12	13
17	18	19	20
24	25	26	27

January 2022

FRIDAY	SATURDAY	SUNDAY	NOTES
	1	2	○
			○
			○
			○
			○
7	8	9	○
			○
			○
			○
14	15	16	○
			○
			○
			○
			○
21	22	23	○
			○
			○
			○
			○
28	29	30	31

February 2022

MONDAY	TUESDAY	WEDNESDAY	THURSDAY
	1	2	3
7	8	9	10
14	15	16	17
21	22	23	24
28			

February 2022

FRIDAY	SATURDAY	SUNDAY	NOTES
4	5	6	○
			○
			○
			○
			○
11	12	13	○
			○
			○
			○
18	19	20	○
			○
			○
			○
			○
25	26	27	○
			○
			○
			○
			○
			NOTES

March 2022

MONDAY	TUESDAY	WEDNESDAY	THURSDAY
	1	2	3
7	8	9	10
14	15	16	17
21	22	23	24
28	29	30	31

March 2022

FRIDAY	SATURDAY	SUNDAY	NOTES
4	5	6	○
			○
			○
			○
			○
11	12	13	○
			○
			○
			○
18	19	20	○
			○
			○
			○
25	26	27	○
			○
			○
			○
			○
			NOTES

MONDAY	TUESDAY	WEDNESDAY	THURSDAY
4	5	6	7
11	12	13	14
18	19	20	21
25	26	27	28

April 2022

FRIDAY	SATURDAY	SUNDAY	NOTES
1	2	3	○
			○
			○
			○
			○
8	9	10	○
			○
			○
			○
15	16	17	○
			○
			○
			○
22	23	24	○
			○
			○
			○
			○
29	30	1	NOTES

May

MONDAY	TUESDAY	WEDNESDAY	THURSDAY
2	3	4	5
9	10	11	12
16	17	18	19
23	24	25	26
30	31		

May 2022

FRIDAY	SATURDAY	SUNDAY	NOTES
6	7	8	○
			○
			○
			○
			○
13	14	15	○
			○
			○
			○
			○
20	21	22	○
			○
			○
			○
			○
27	28	29	○
			○
			○
			○
			○
			NOTES

June 2022

MONDAY	TUESDAY	WEDNESDAY	THURSDAY
		1	2
6	7	8	9
13	14	15	16
20	21	22	23
27	28	29	30

June 2022

FRIDAY	SATURDAY	SUNDAY	NOTES
3	4	5	○
			○
			○
			○
			○
10	11	12	○
			○
			○
			○
17	18	19	○
			○
			○
			○
			○
24	25	26	○
			○
			○
			○
			○
			NOTES

July 2022

MONDAY	TUESDAY	WEDNESDAY	THURSDAY
4	5	6	7
11	12	13	14
18	19	20	21
25	26	27	28

July 2022

FRIDAY	SATURDAY	SUNDAY	NOTES
1	2	3	○
			○
			○
			○
8	9	10	○
			○
			○
			○
15	16	17	○
			○
			○
			○
22	23	24	○
			○
			○
			○
			○
29	30	31	NOTES

August 2022

MONDAY	TUESDAY	WEDNESDAY	THURSDAY
1	2	3	4
8	9	10	11
15	16	17	18
22	23	24	25
29	30	31	

August 2022

FRIDAY	SATURDAY	SUNDAY	NOTES
5	6	7	○
			○
			○
			○
12	13	14	○
			○
			○
			○
19	20	21	○
			○
			○
			○
			○
26	27	28	NOTES

September 2022

MONDAY	TUESDAY	WEDNESDAY	THURSDAY
			1
5	6	7	8
12	13	14	15
19	20	21	22
26	27	28	29

September 2022

FRIDAY	SATURDAY	SUNDAY	NOTES
2	3	4	○
			○
			○
			○
			○
9	10	11	○
			○
			○
			○
16	17	18	○
			○
			○
			○
			○
23	24	25	○
			○
			○
			○
			○
30			NOTES

October 2022

MONDAY	TUESDAY	WEDNESDAY	THURSDAY
3	4	5	6
10	11	12	13
17	18	19	20
24	25	26	27

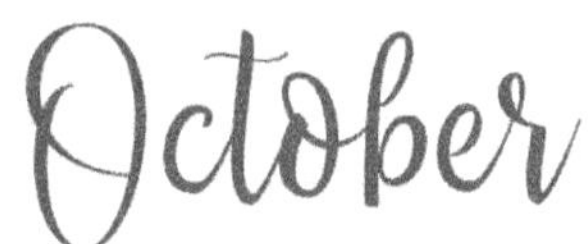

October 2022

FRIDAY	SATURDAY	SUNDAY	NOTES
	1	2	○
			○
			○
			○
			○
7	8	9	○
			○
			○
			○
14	15	16	○
			○
			○
			○
			○
21	22	23	○
			○
			○
			○
			○
28	29	30	NOTES
		31 MONDAY	

November 2022

MONDAY	TUESDAY	WEDNESDAY	THURSDAY
	1	2	3
7	8	9	10
14	15	16	17
21	22	23	24
28	29	30	

November 2022

FRIDAY	SATURDAY	SUNDAY	NOTES
4	5	6	○
			○
			○
			○
			○
11	12	13	○
			○
			○
			○
18	19	20	○
			○
			○
			○
			○
25	26	27	○
			○
			○
			○
			○
			NOTES

December 2022

MONDAY	TUESDAY	WEDNESDAY	THURSDAY
			1
5	6	7	8
12	13	14	15
19	20	21	22
26	27	28	29

December 2022

FRIDAY	SATURDAY	SUNDAY	NOTES
2	3	4	○
			○
			○
			○
			○
9	10	11	○
			○
			○
			○
16	17	18	○
			○
			○
			○
			○
23	24	25	○
			○
			○
			○
			○
30	31		NOTES

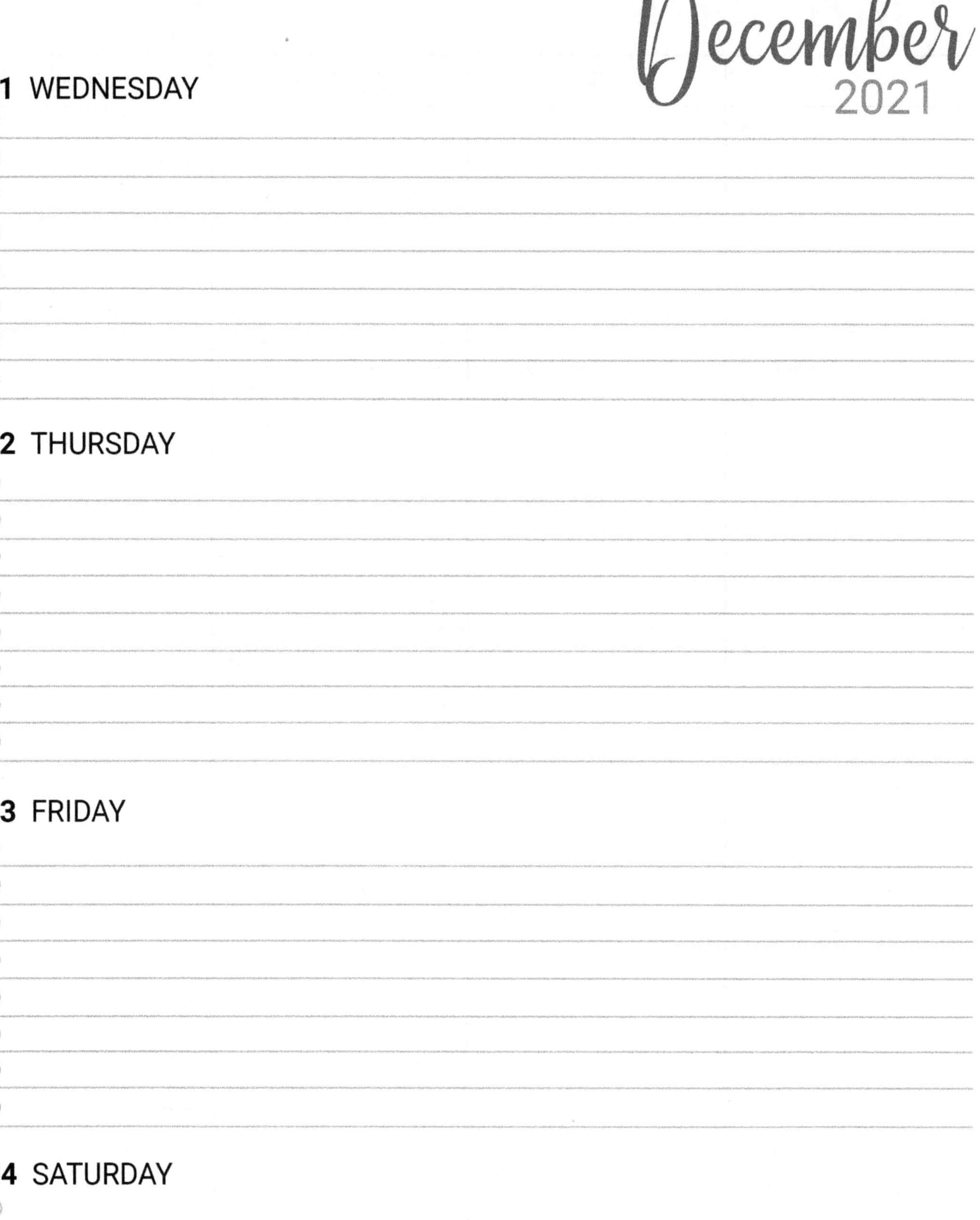

December
2021

01 WEDNESDAY

02 THURSDAY

03 FRIDAY

04 SATURDAY

December
2021

05 SUNDAY

06 MONDAY

07 TUESDAY

08 WEDNESDAY

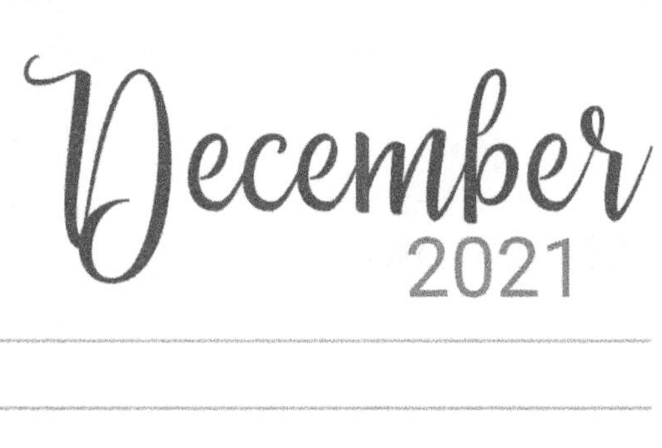

December
2021

09 THURSDAY

10 FRIDAY

11 SATURDAY

12 SUNDAY

13 MONDAY

14 TUESDAY

15 WEDNESDAY

16 THURSDAY

17 FRIDAY

18 SATURDAY

19 SUNDAY

20 MONDAY

21 TUESDAY

○
○
○
○
○
○
○
○

22 WEDNESDAY

○
○
○
○
○
○
○
○
○

23 THURSDAY

○
○
○
○
○
○
○
○

24 FRIDAY

○
○
○
○
○

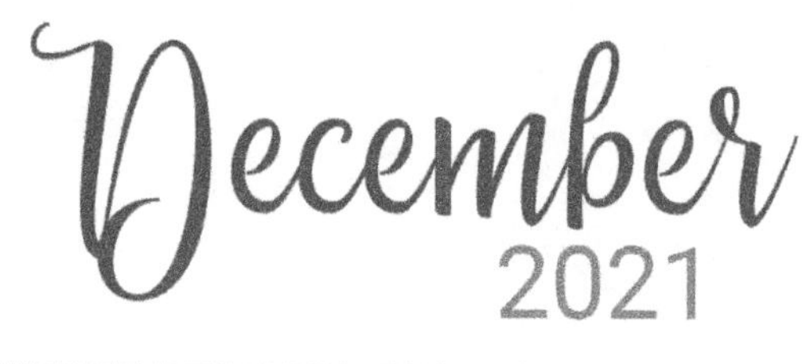

25 SATURDAY

26 SUNDAY

27 MONDAY

28 TUESDAY

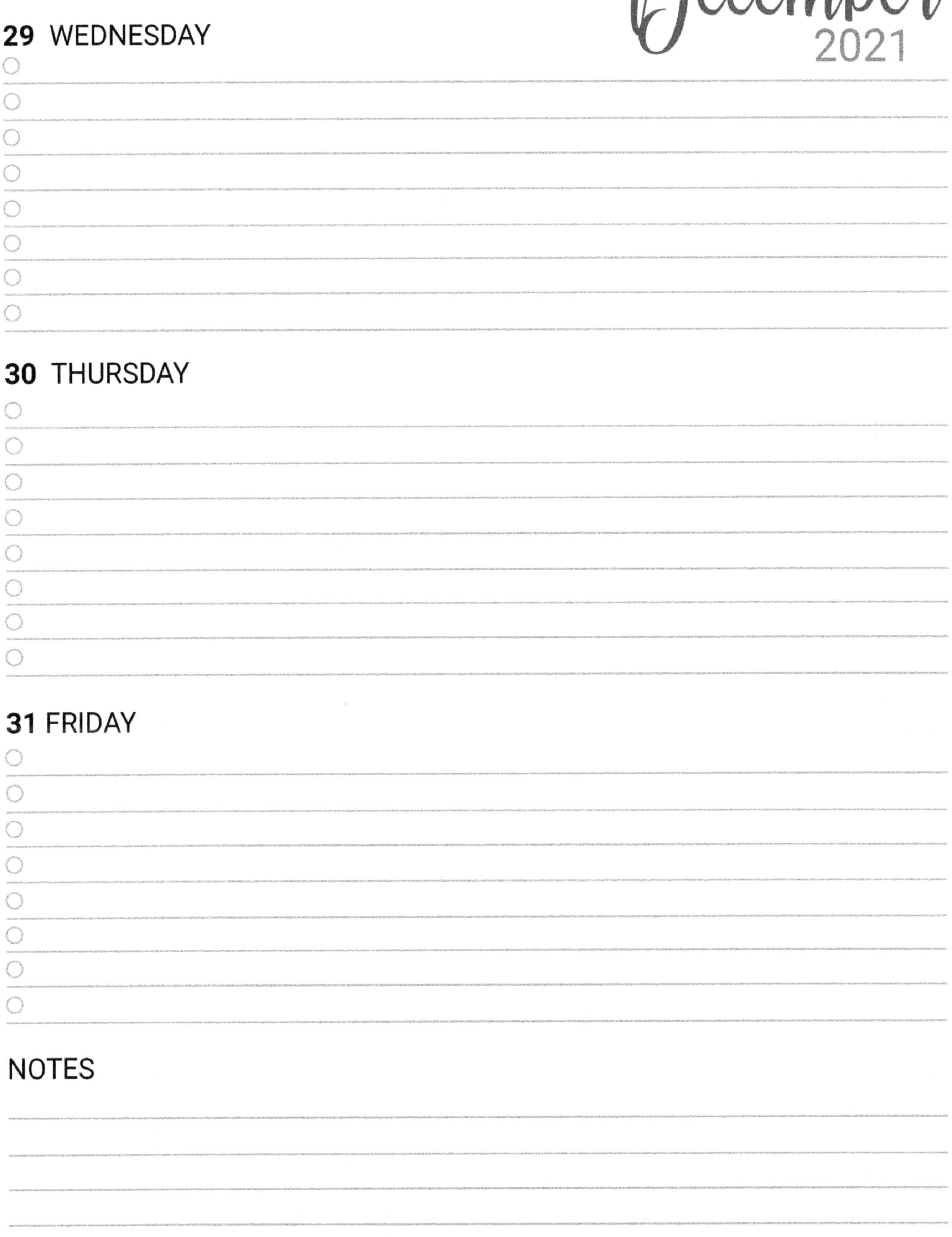

29 WEDNESDAY

30 THURSDAY

31 FRIDAY

NOTES

January
2022

01 SATURDAY

○
○
○
○
○
○
○
○

02 SUNDAY

○
○
○
○
○
○
○
○

03 MONDAY

○
○
○
○
○
○
○
○

04 TUESDAY

○
○
○
○
○

January
2022

05 WEDNESDAY

-
-
-
-
-
-
-

06 THURSDAY

-
-
-
-
-
-
-
-

07 FRIDAY

-
-
-
-
-
-
-

08 SATURDAY

-
-
-
-
-

09 SUNDAY

10 MONDAY

11 TUESDAY

12 WEDNESDAY

13 THURSDAY

14 FRIDAY

15 SATURDAY

16 SUNDAY

17 MONDAY

18 TUESDAY

19 WEDNESDAY

20 THURSDAY

January
2022

21 FRIDAY

22 SATURDAY

23 SUNDAY

24 MONDAY

25 TUESDAY

26 WEDNESDAY

27 THURSDAY

28 FRIDAY

29 SATURDAY

○
○
○
○
○
○
○
○

30 SUNDAY

○
○
○
○
○
○
○
○

31 MONDAY

○
○
○
○
○
○
○
○

NOTES

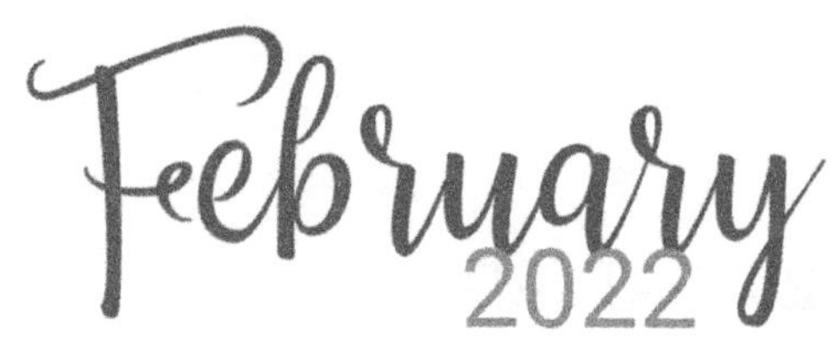

01 TUESDAY

02 WEDNESDAY

03 THURSDAY

04 FRIDAY

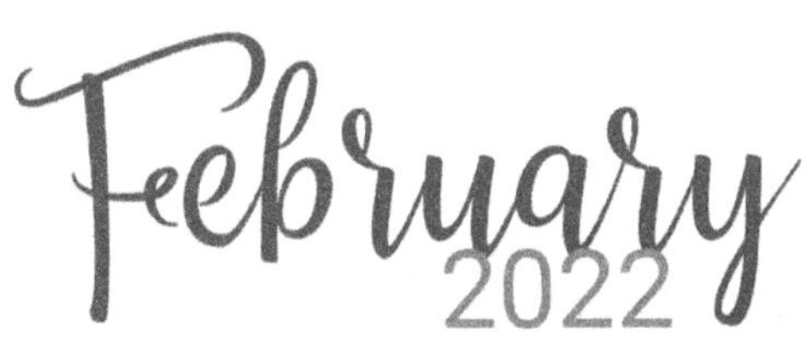

05 SATURDAY

06 SUNDAY

07 MONDAY

08 TUESDAY

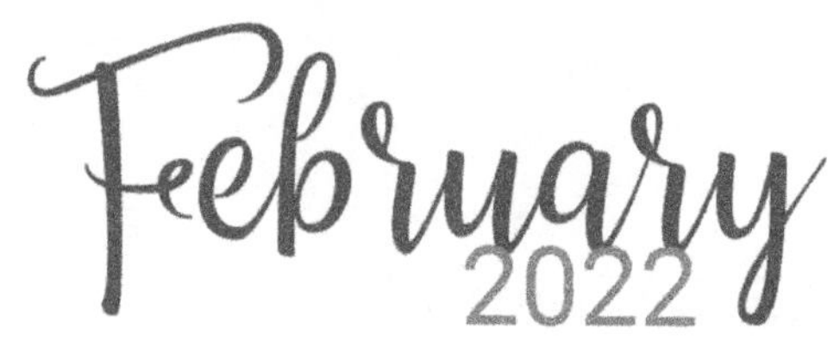

09 WEDNESDAY

10 THURSDAY

11 FRIDAY

12 SATURDAY

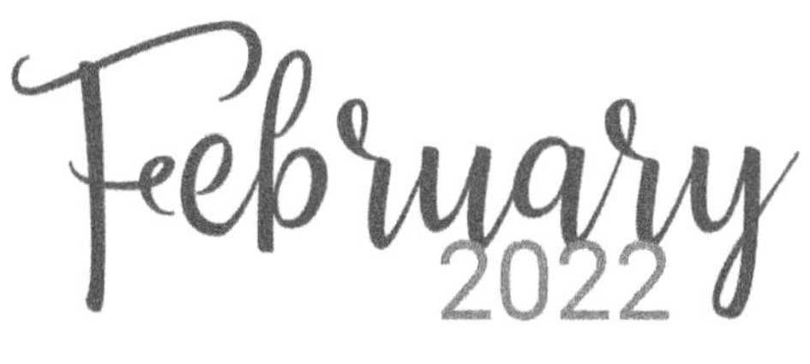

February 2022

13 SUNDAY

14 MONDAY

15 TUESDAY

16 WEDNESDAY

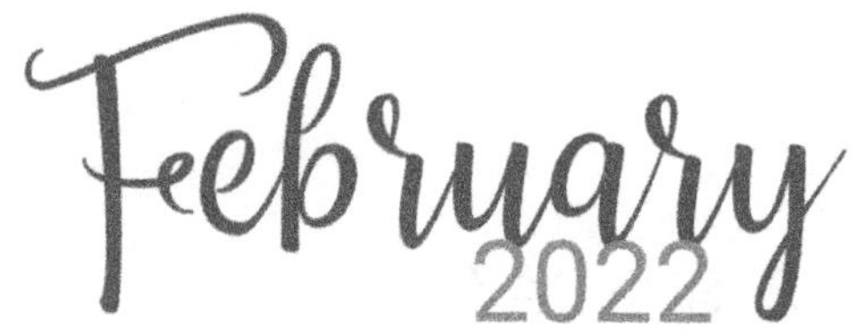

February
2022

17 THURSDAY

18 FRIDAY

19 SATURDAY

20 SUNDAY

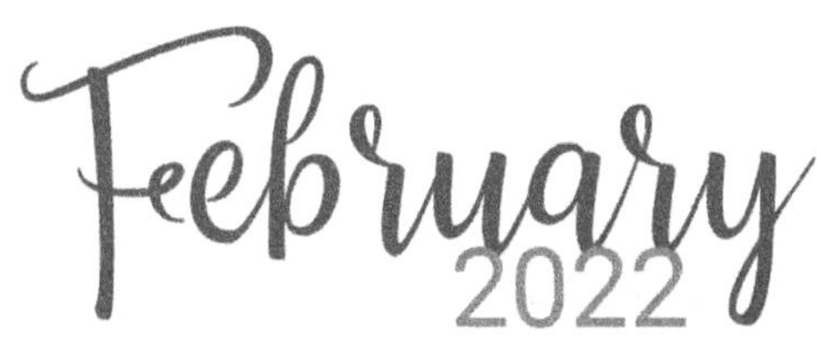

21 MONDAY

22 TUESDAY

23 WEDNESDAY

24 THURSDAY

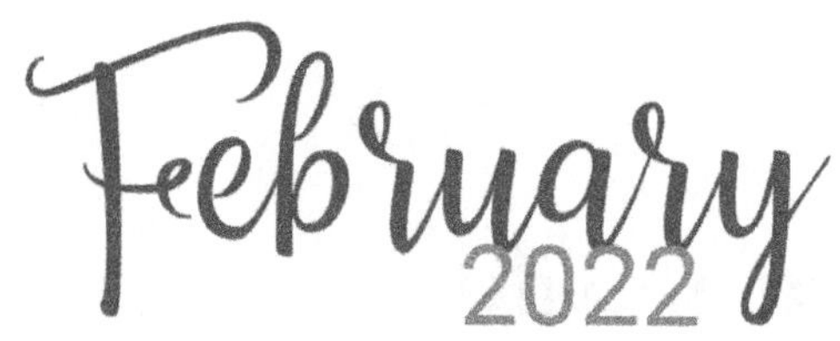

25 FRIDAY

26 SATURDAY

27 SUNDAY

28 MONDAY

01 TUESDAY

02 WEDNESDAY

03 THURSDAY

04 FRIDAY

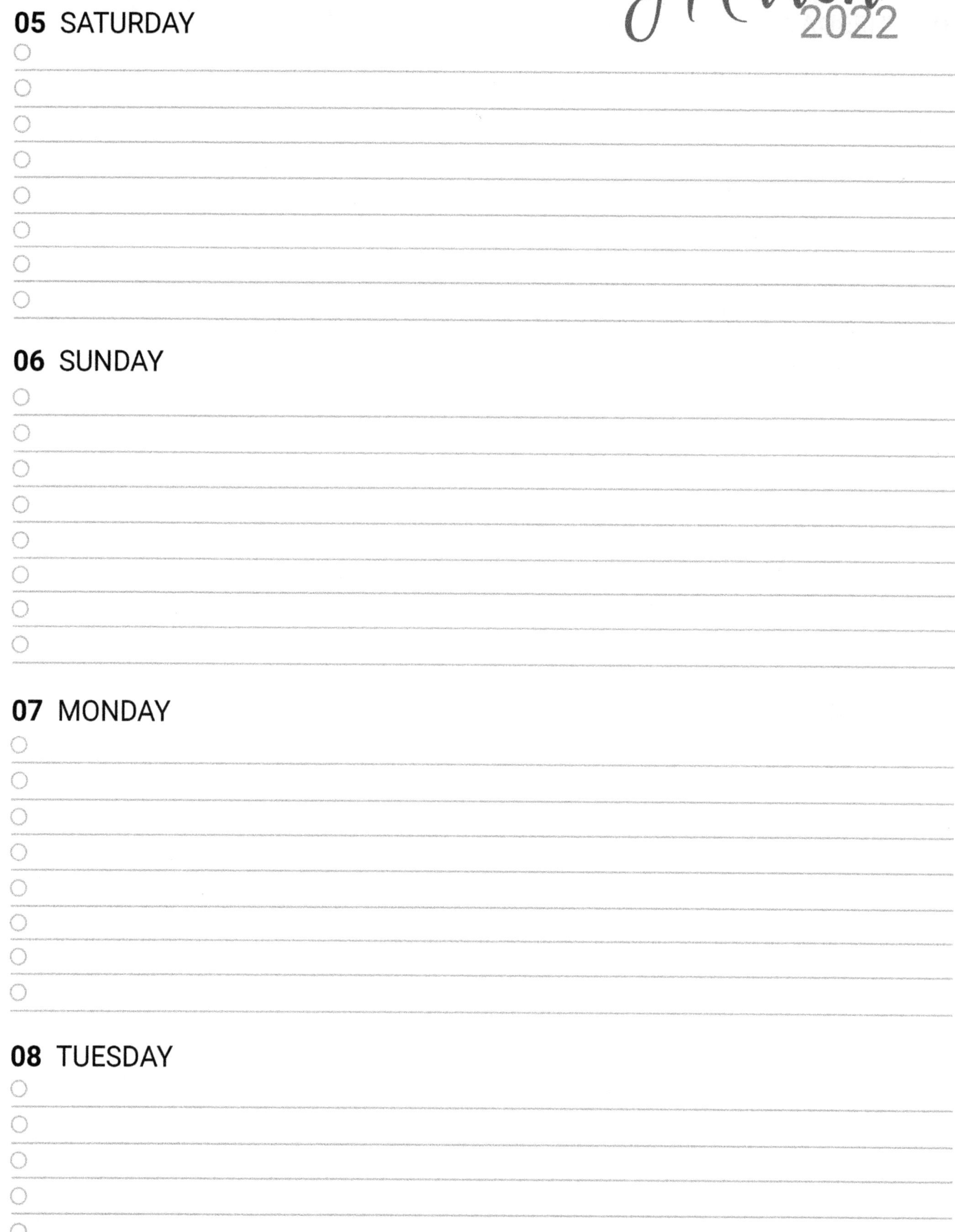

March 2022

05 SATURDAY

06 SUNDAY

07 MONDAY

08 TUESDAY

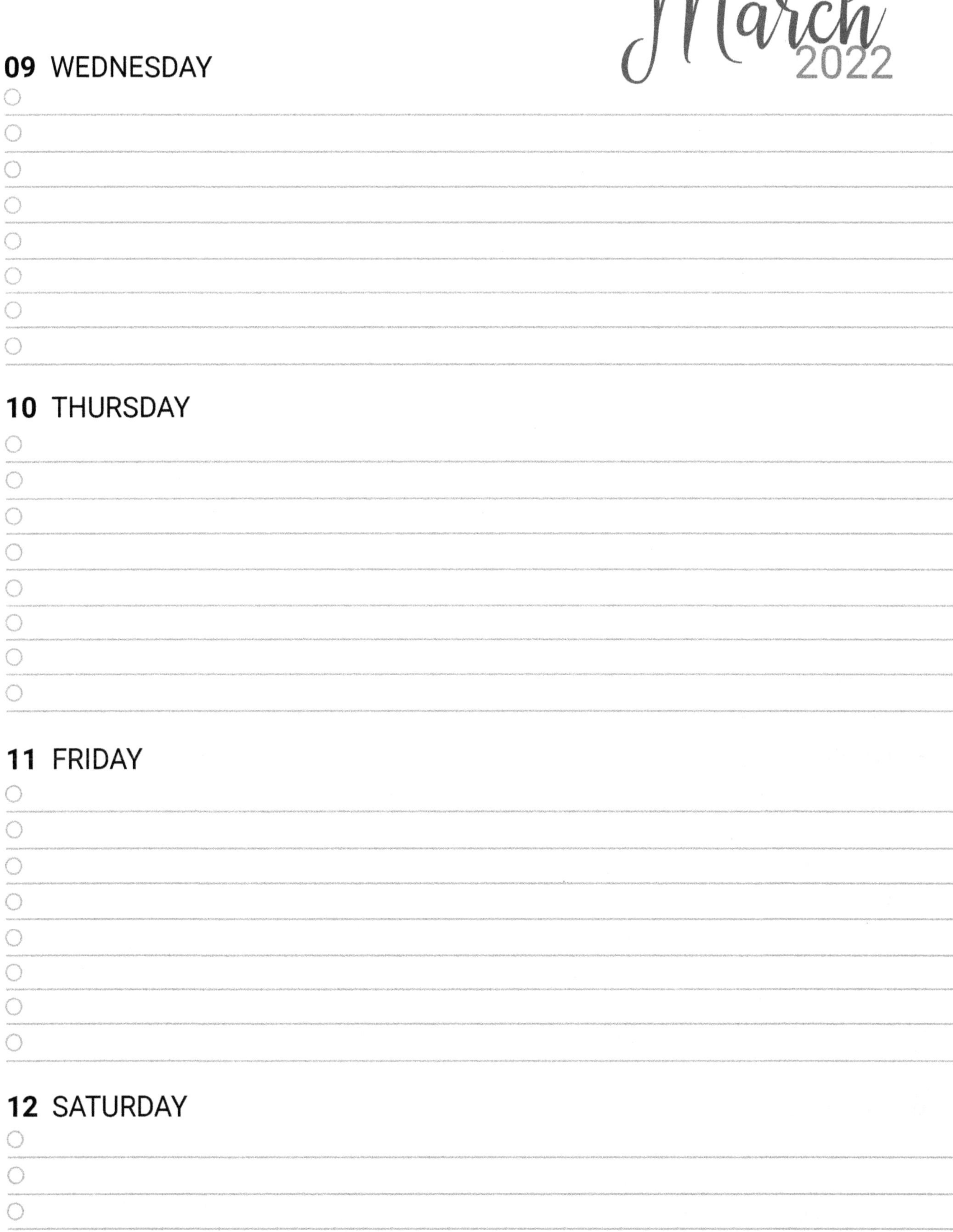

09 WEDNESDAY

10 THURSDAY

11 FRIDAY

12 SATURDAY

March 2022

13 SUNDAY

14 MONDAY

15 TUESDAY

16 WEDNESDAY

17 THURSDAY

18 FRIDAY

19 SATURDAY

20 SUNDAY

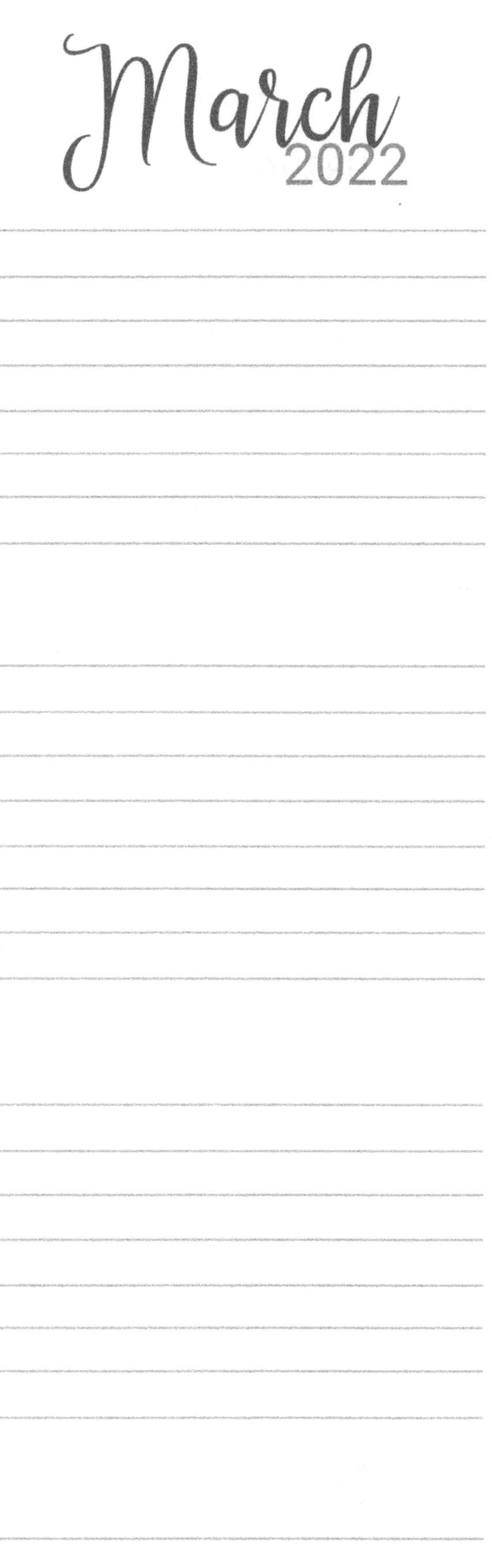

21 MONDAY

22 TUESDAY

23 WEDNESDAY

24 THURSDAY

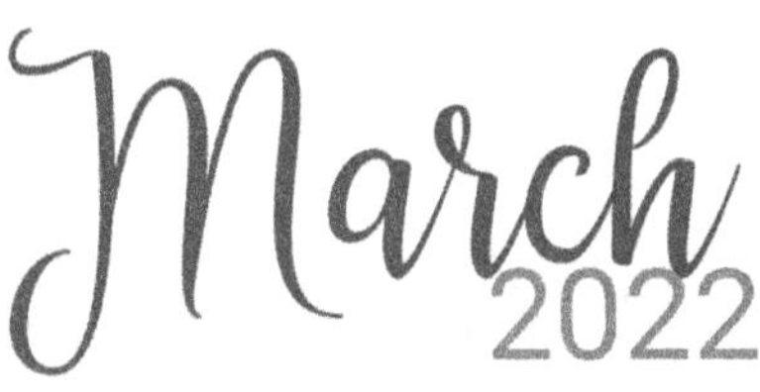

25 FRIDAY

26 SATURDAY

27 SUNDAY

28 MONDAY

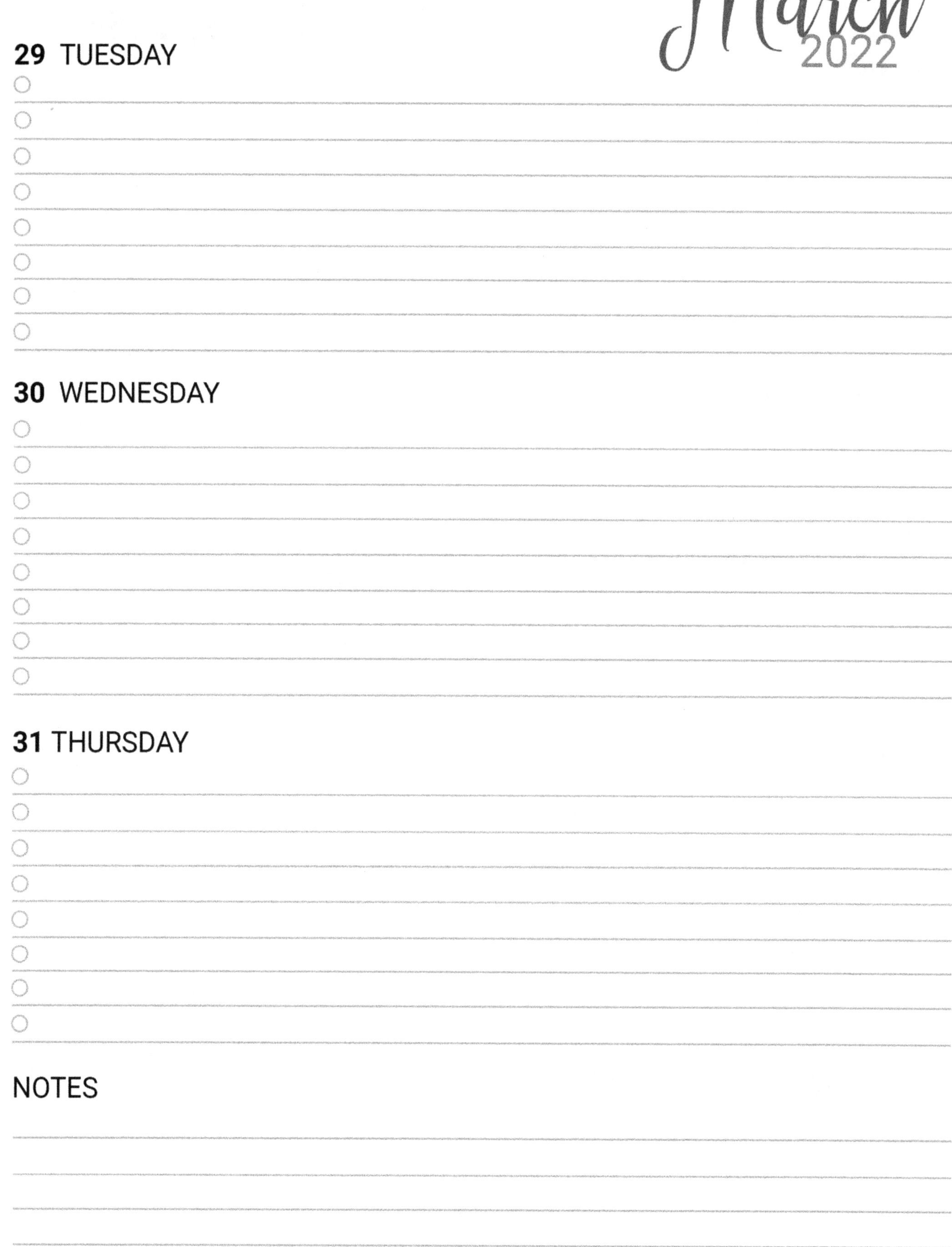

29 TUESDAY

30 WEDNESDAY

31 THURSDAY

NOTES

01 FRIDAY

02 SATURDAY

03 SUNDAY

04 MONDAY

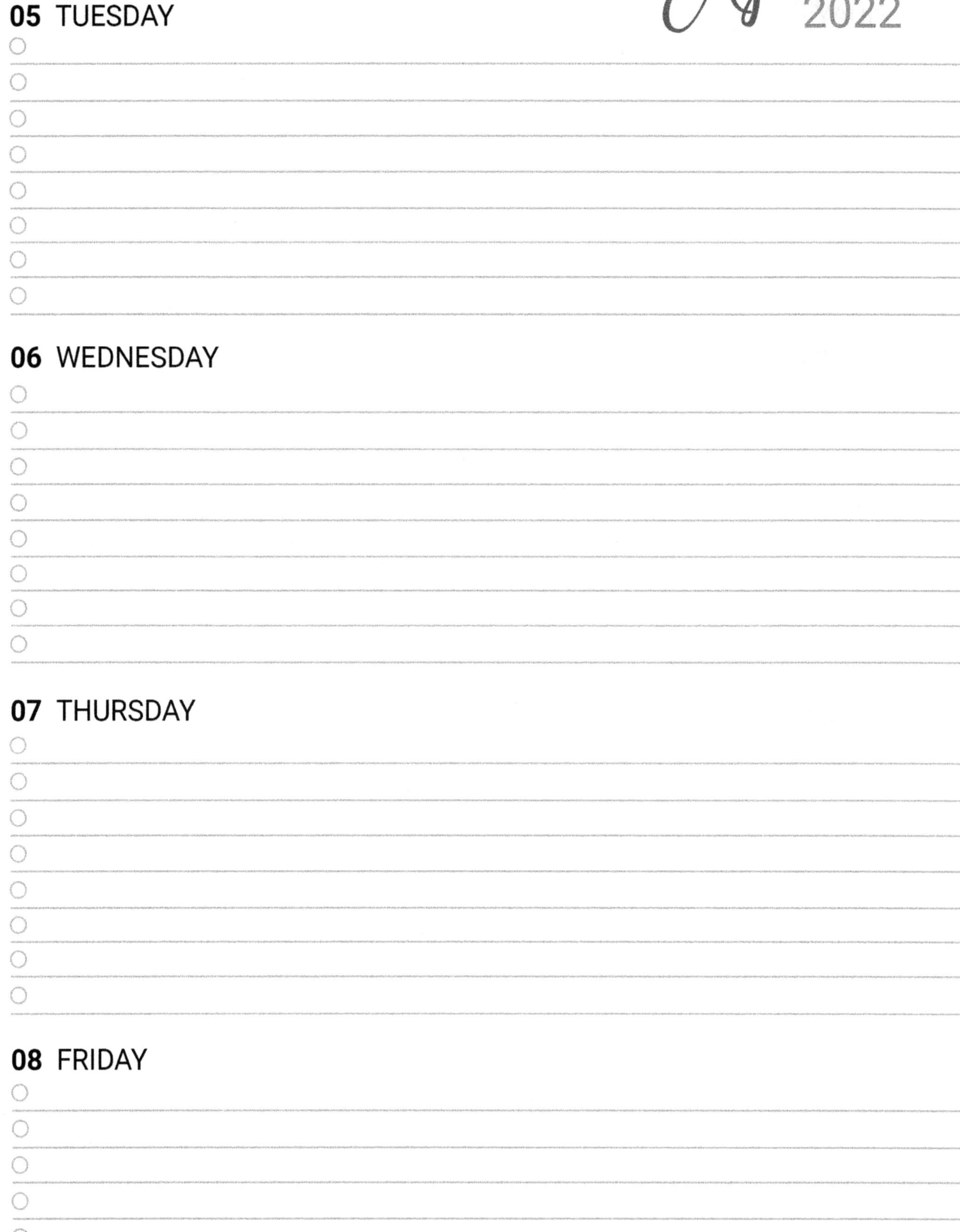

April
2022

05 TUESDAY

06 WEDNESDAY

07 THURSDAY

08 FRIDAY

09 SATURDAY

10 SUNDAY

11 MONDAY

12 TUESDAY

13 WEDNESDAY

14 THURSDAY

15 FRIDAY

16 SATURDAY

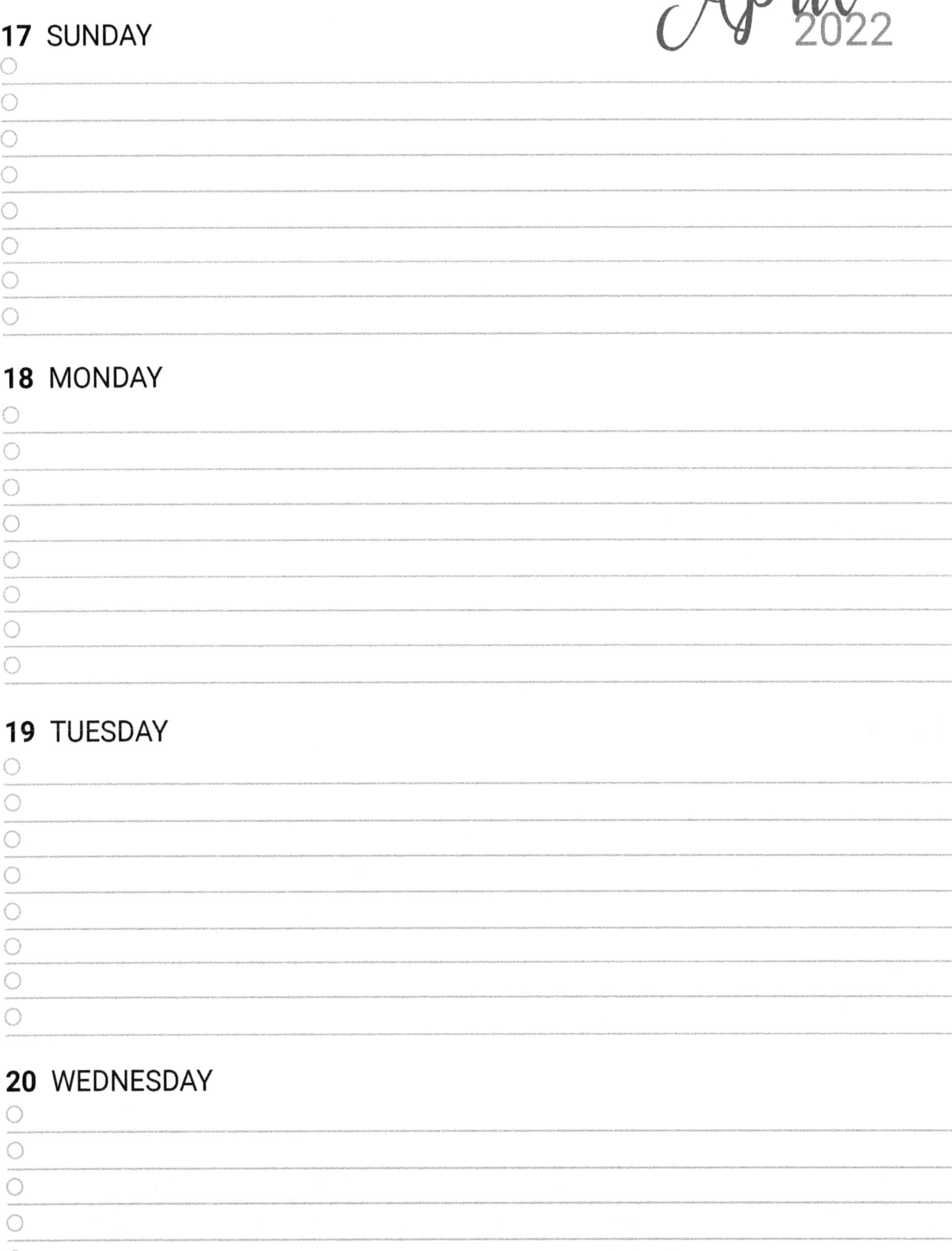

17 SUNDAY

18 MONDAY

19 TUESDAY

20 WEDNESDAY

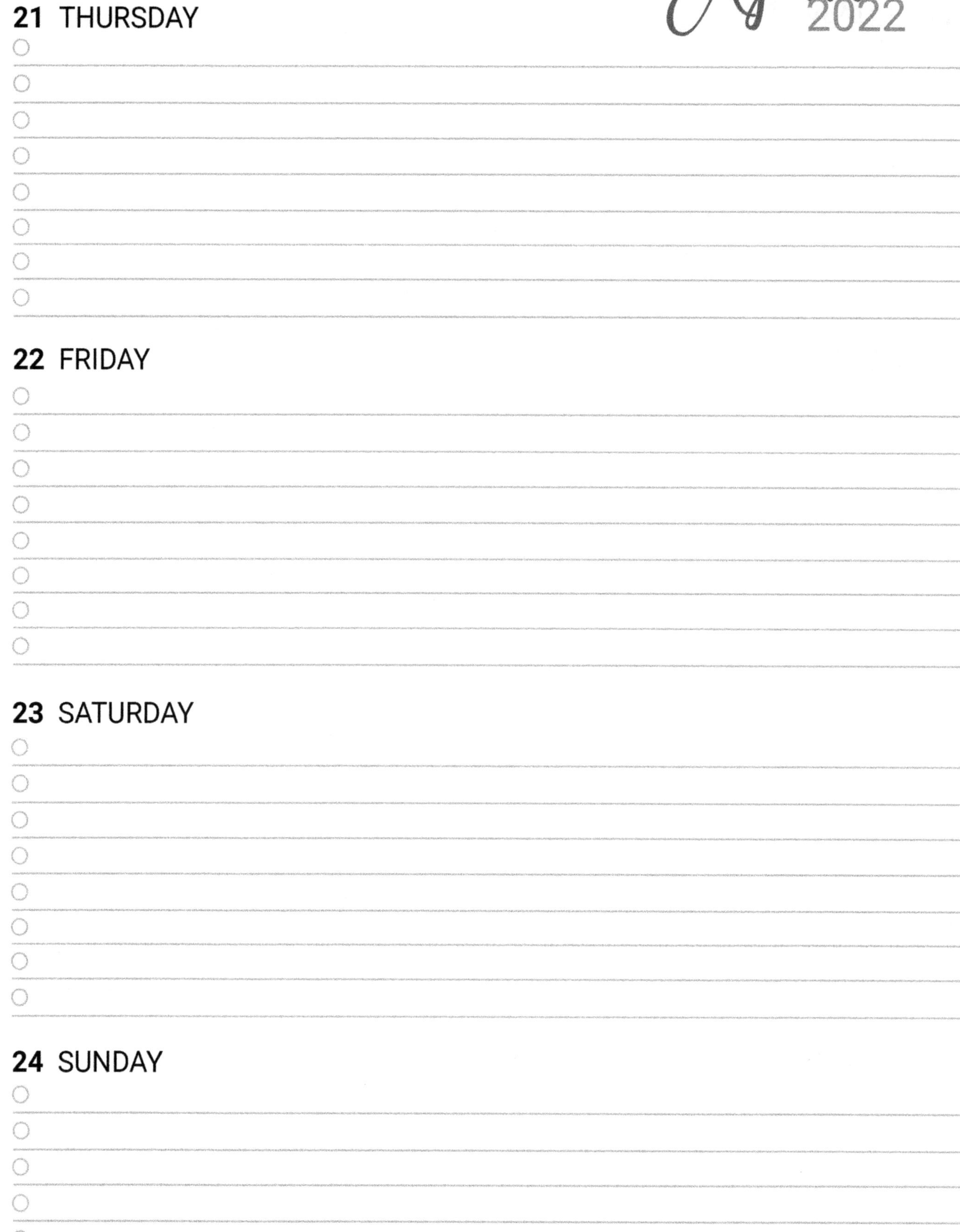

April
2022

21 THURSDAY

22 FRIDAY

23 SATURDAY

24 SUNDAY

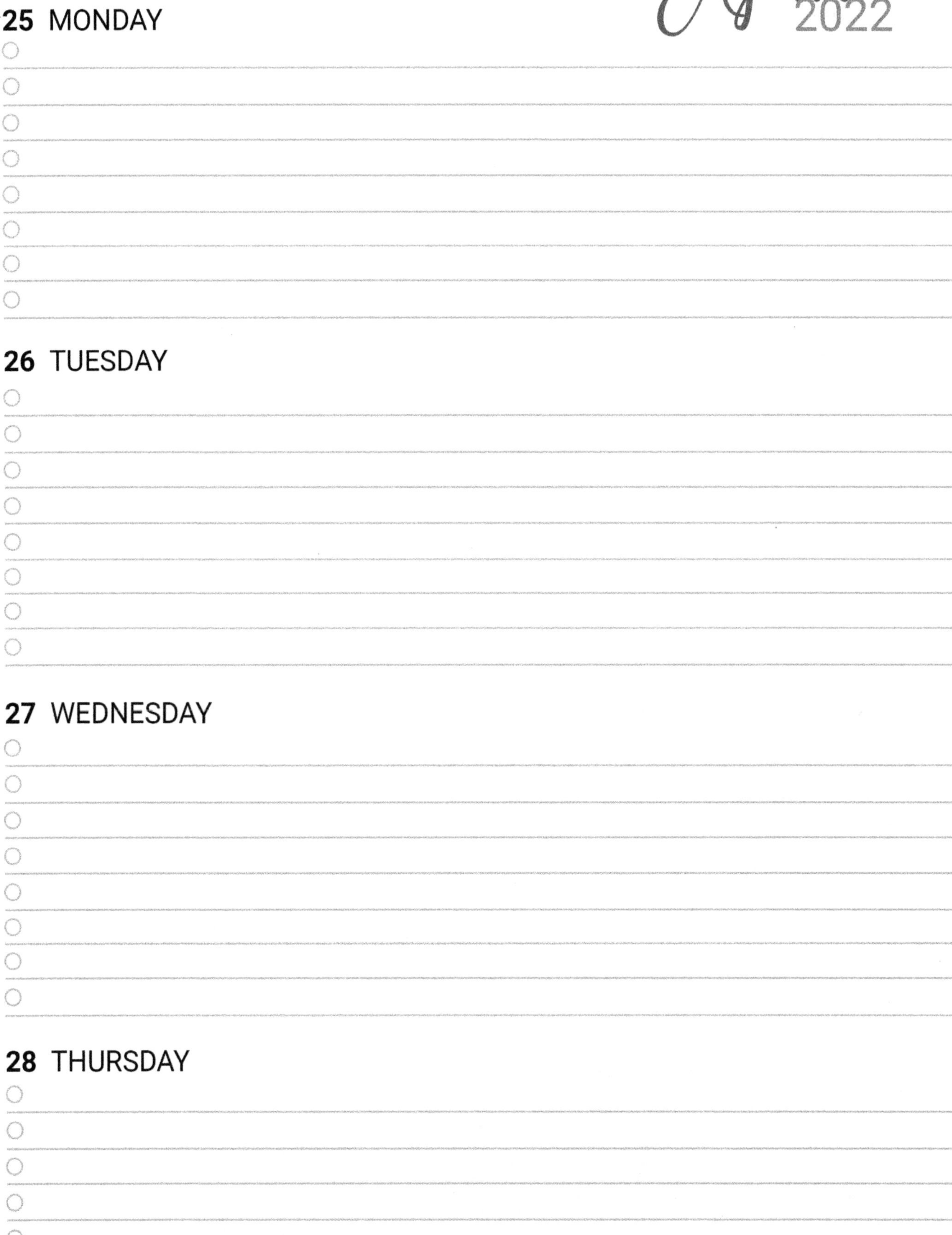

25 MONDAY

26 TUESDAY

27 WEDNESDAY

28 THURSDAY

29 FRIDAY

○ ____
○ ____
○ ____
○ ____
○ ____
○ ____
○ ____
○ ____

30 SATURDAY

○ ____
○ ____
○ ____
○ ____
○ ____
○ ____
○ ____
○ ____

NOTES

May
2022

01 SUNDAY

02 MONDAY

03 TUESDAY

04 WEDNESDAY

05 THURSDAY

06 FRIDAY

07 SATURDAY

08 SUNDAY

09 MONDAY

10 TUESDAY

11 WEDNESDAY

12 THURSDAY

13 FRIDAY

14 SATURDAY

15 SUNDAY

16 MONDAY

17 TUESDAY

18 WEDNESDAY

19 THURSDAY

20 FRIDAY

21 SATURDAY

22 SUNDAY

23 MONDAY

24 TUESDAY

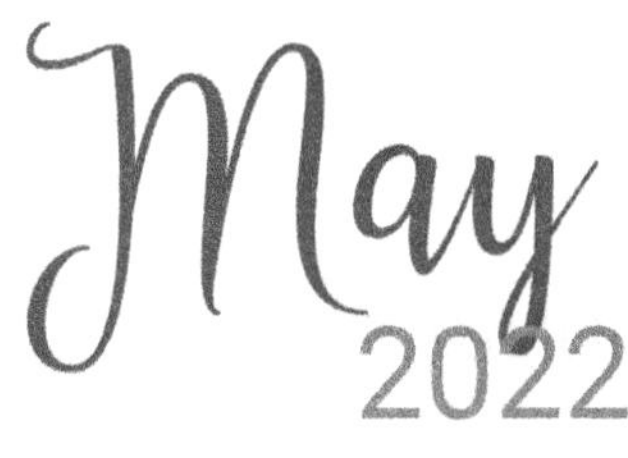

May 2022

25 WEDNESDAY

26 THURSDAY

27 FRIDAY

28 SATURDAY

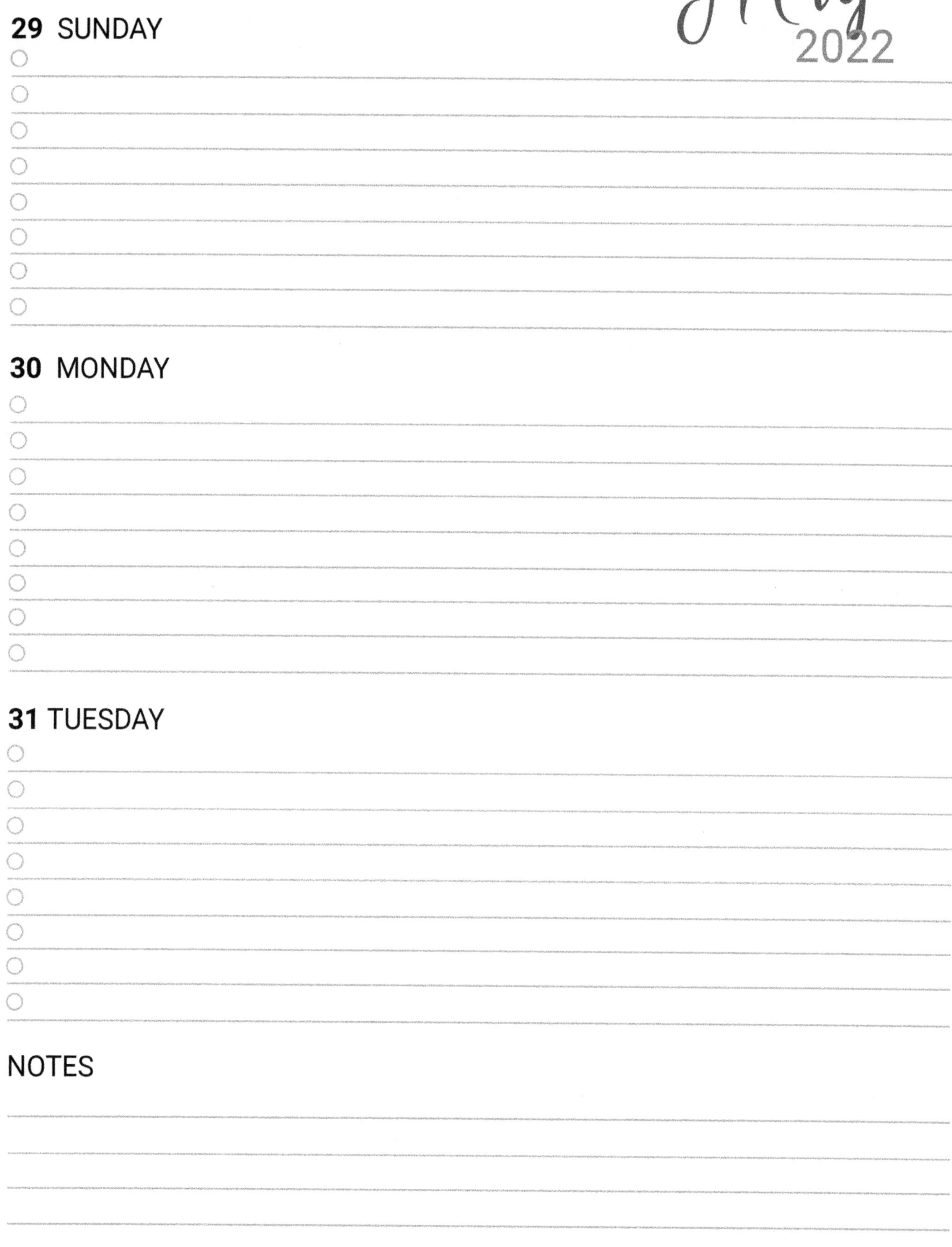

May
2022

29 SUNDAY

30 MONDAY

31 TUESDAY

NOTES

June 2022

01 WEDNESDAY

02 THURSDAY

03 FRIDAY

04 SATURDAY

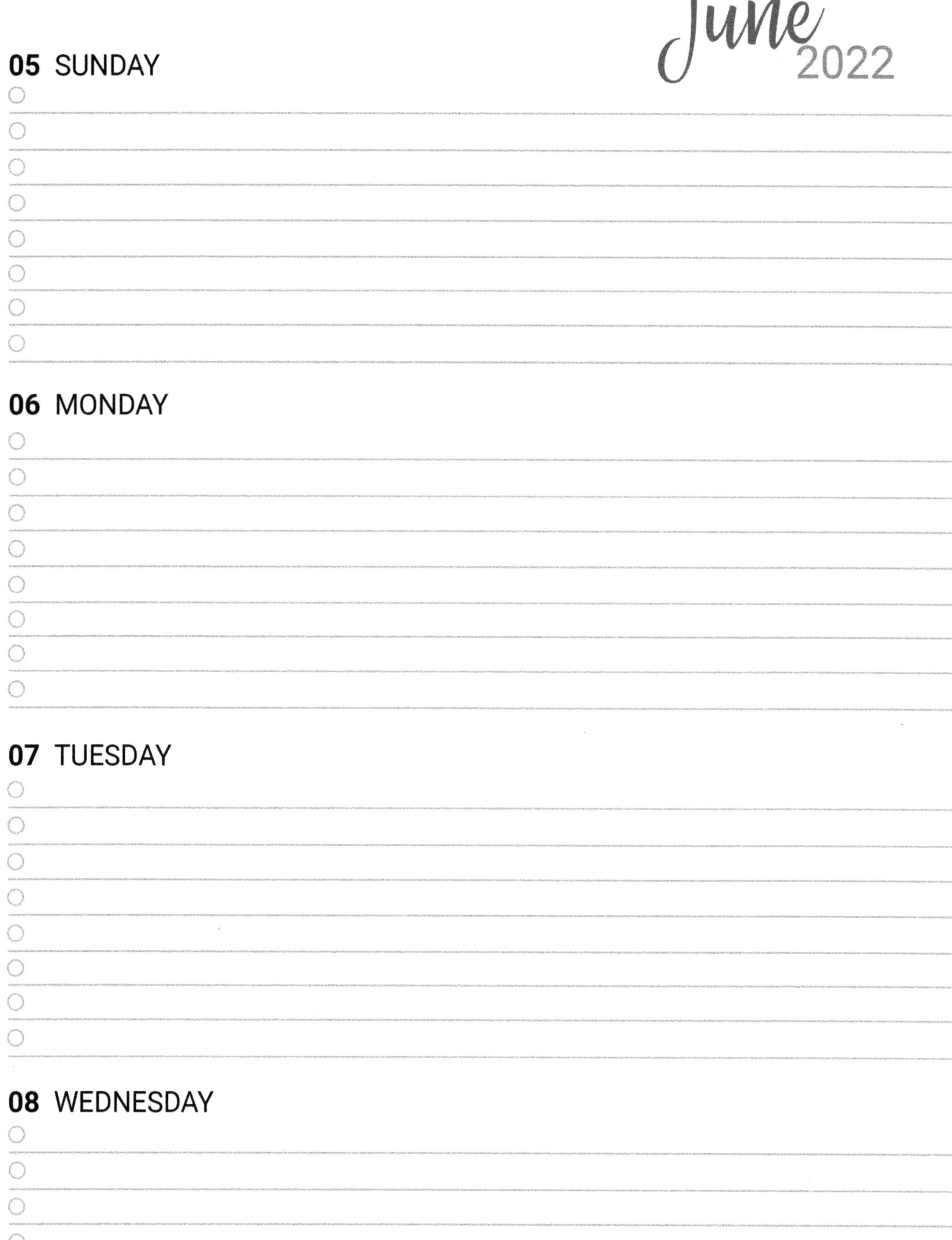

June
2022

05 SUNDAY

06 MONDAY

07 TUESDAY

08 WEDNESDAY

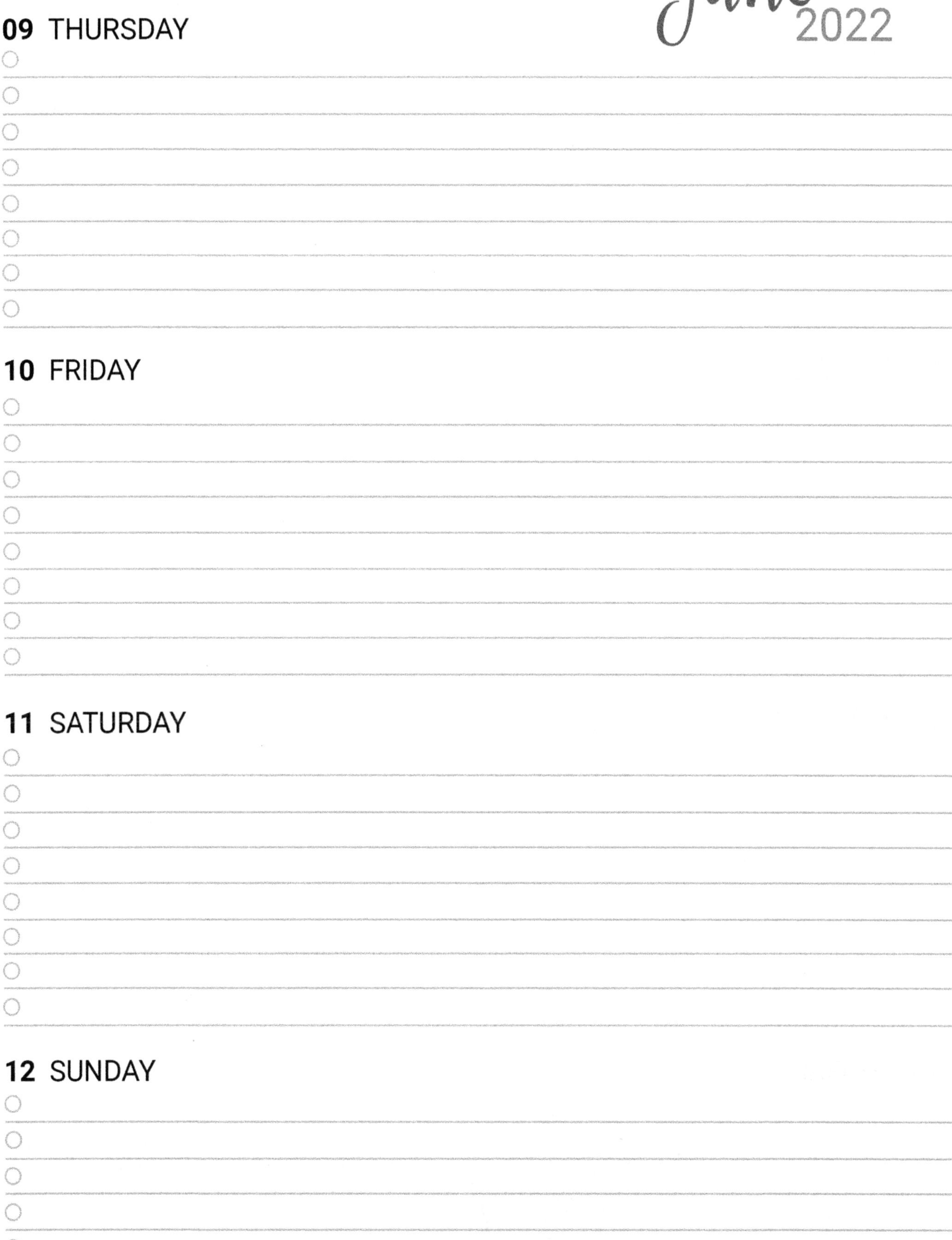

09 THURSDAY

10 FRIDAY

11 SATURDAY

12 SUNDAY

13 MONDAY

14 TUESDAY

15 WEDNESDAY

16 THURSDAY

17 FRIDAY

18 SATURDAY

19 SUNDAY

20 MONDAY

21 TUESDAY

○
○
○
○
○
○
○

22 WEDNESDAY

○
○
○
○
○
○
○
○

23 THURSDAY

○
○
○
○
○
○
○
○

24 FRIDAY

○
○
○
○
○

25 SATURDAY

26 SUNDAY

27 MONDAY

28 TUESDAY

29 WEDNESDAY

30 THURSDAY

NOTES

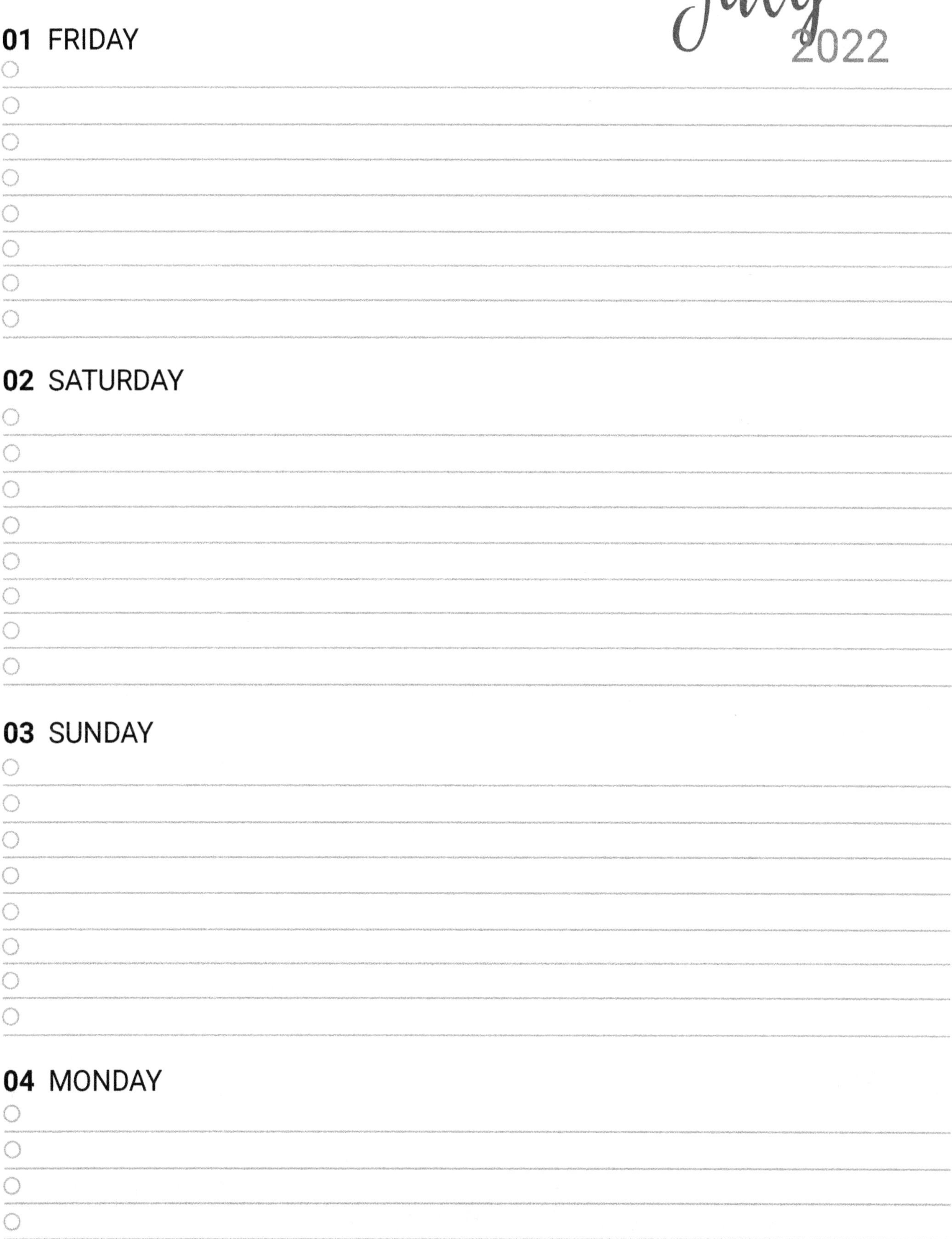

July
2022

01 FRIDAY

02 SATURDAY

03 SUNDAY

04 MONDAY

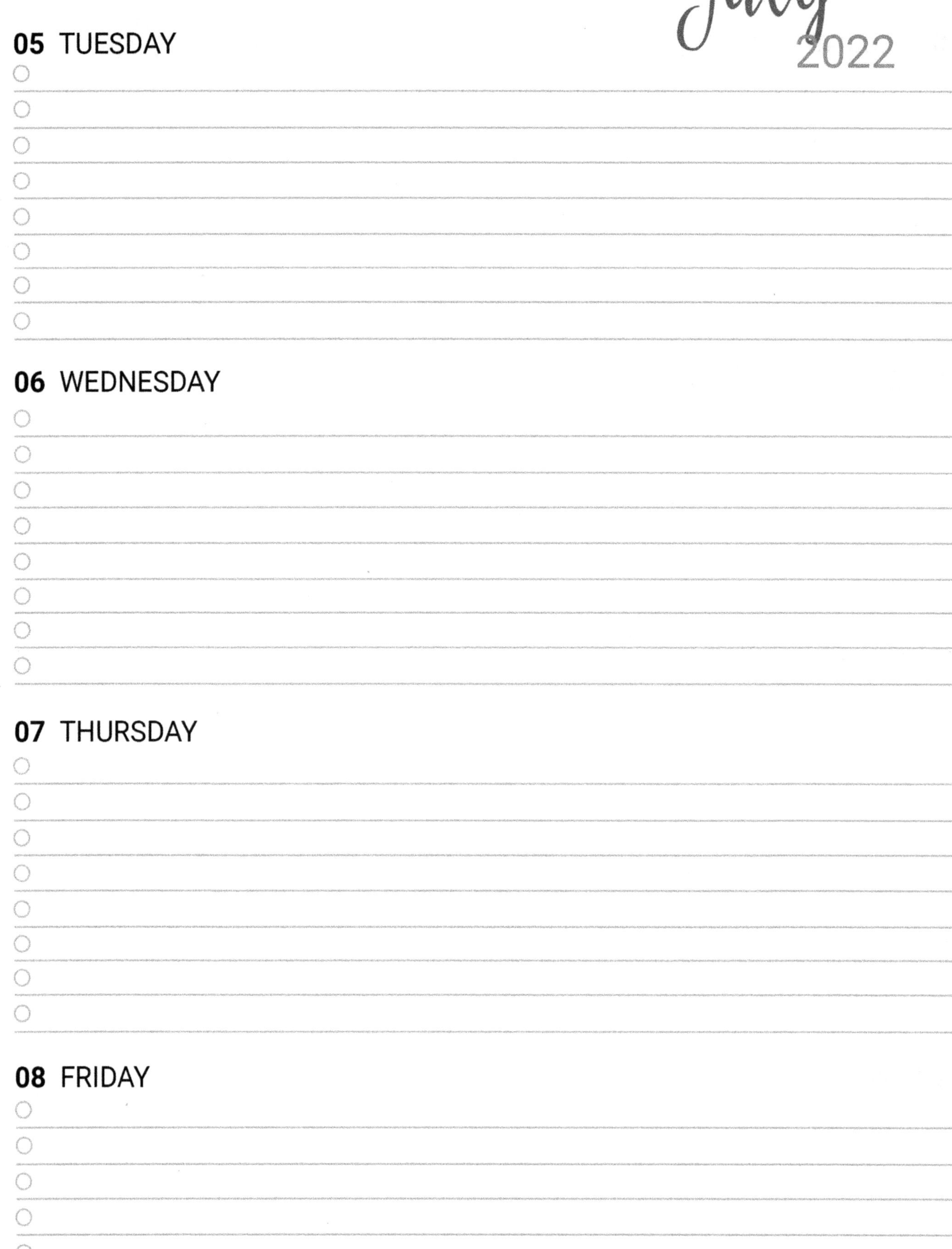

July
2022

05 TUESDAY

06 WEDNESDAY

07 THURSDAY

08 FRIDAY

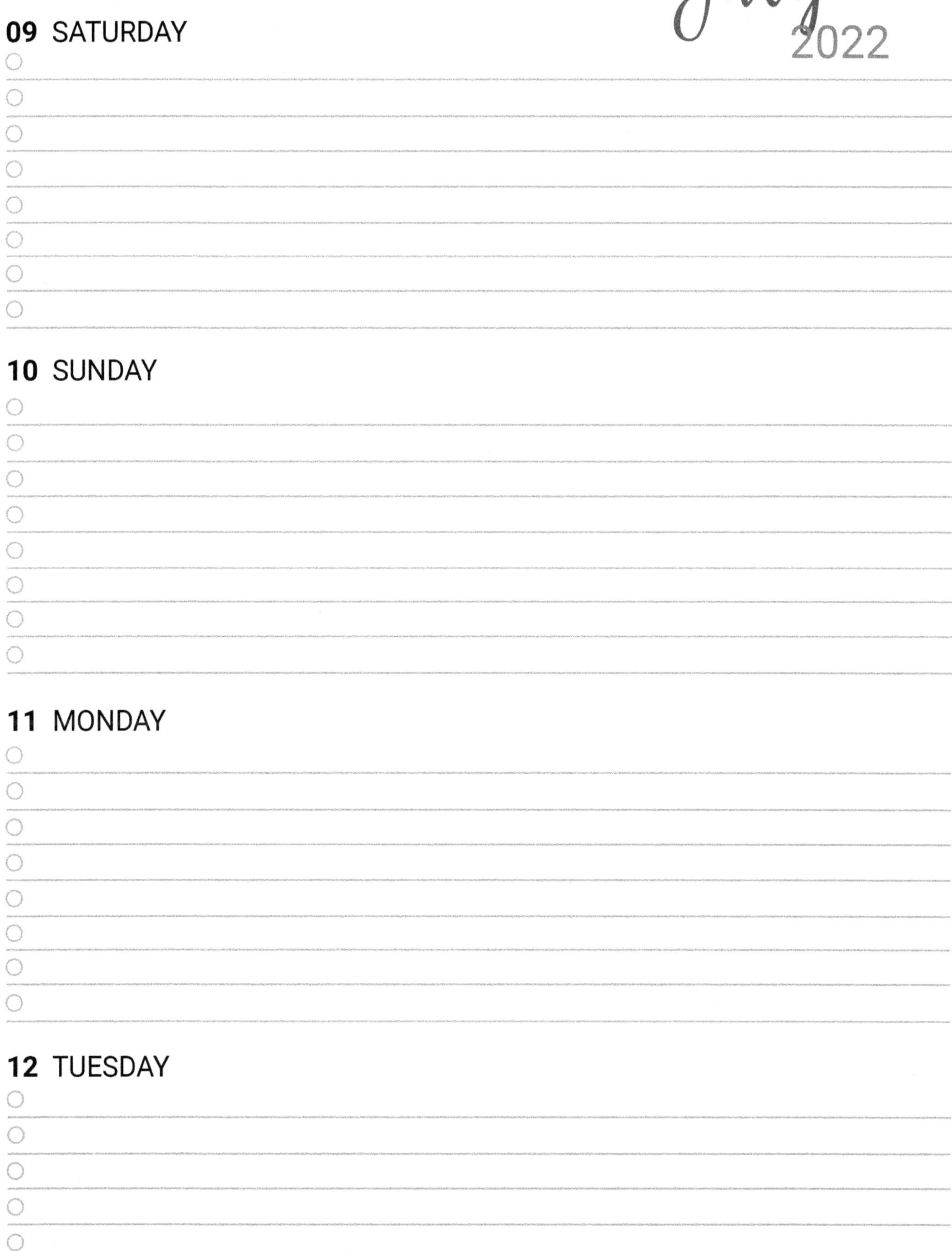

July
2022

09 SATURDAY

10 SUNDAY

11 MONDAY

12 TUESDAY

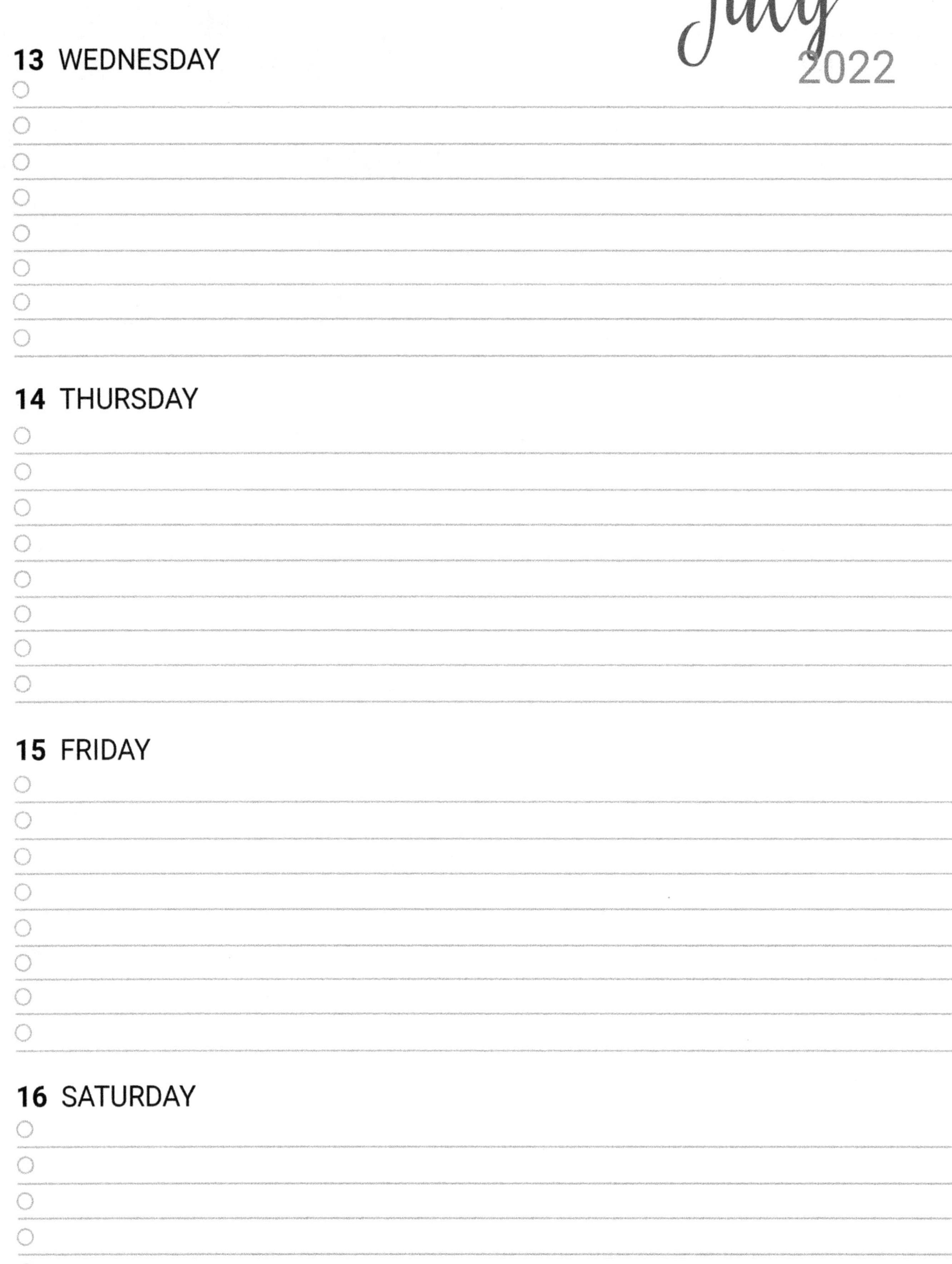

July
2022

13 WEDNESDAY

14 THURSDAY

15 FRIDAY

16 SATURDAY

17 SUNDAY

18 MONDAY

19 TUESDAY

20 WEDNESDAY

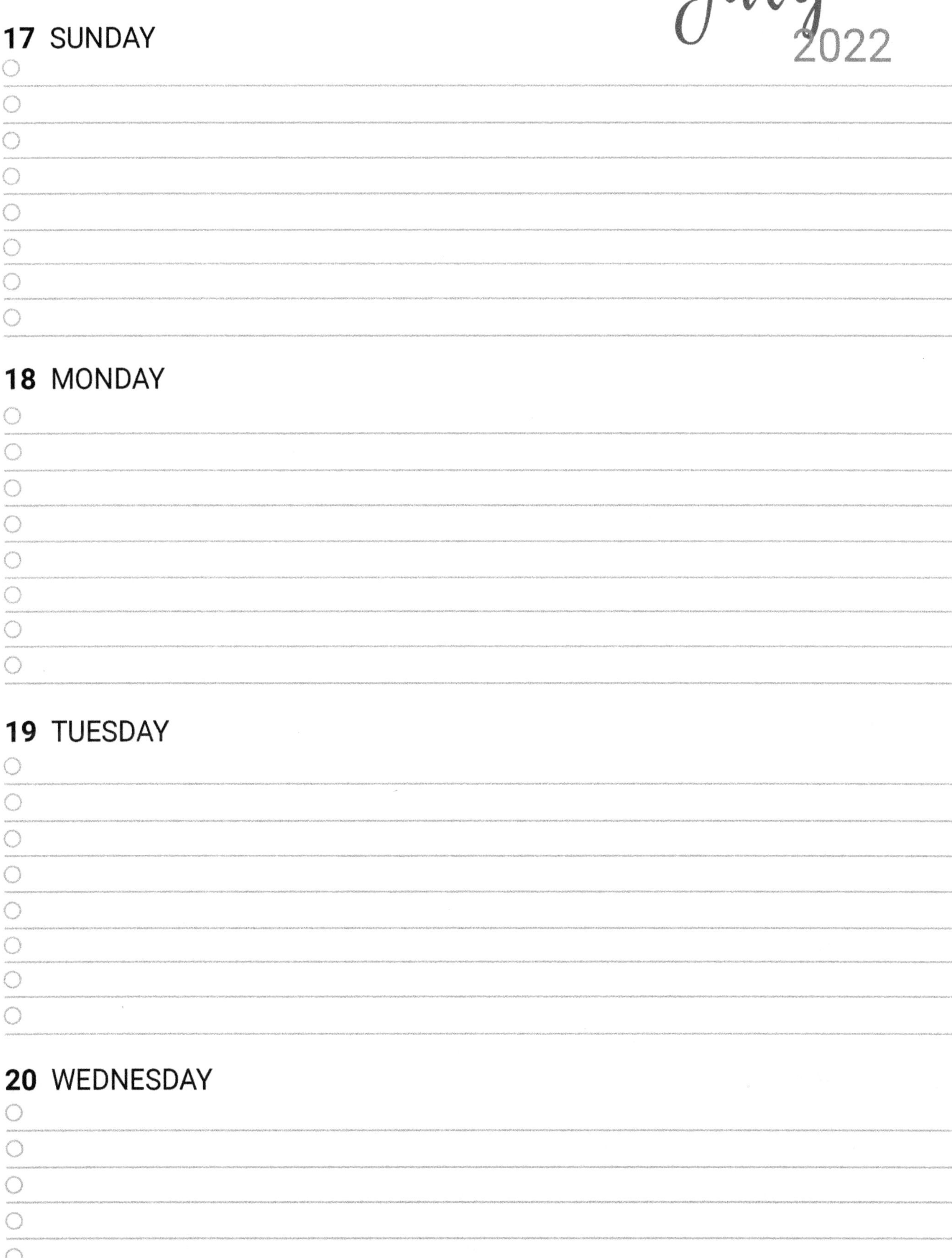

21 THURSDAY

22 FRIDAY

23 SATURDAY

24 SUNDAY

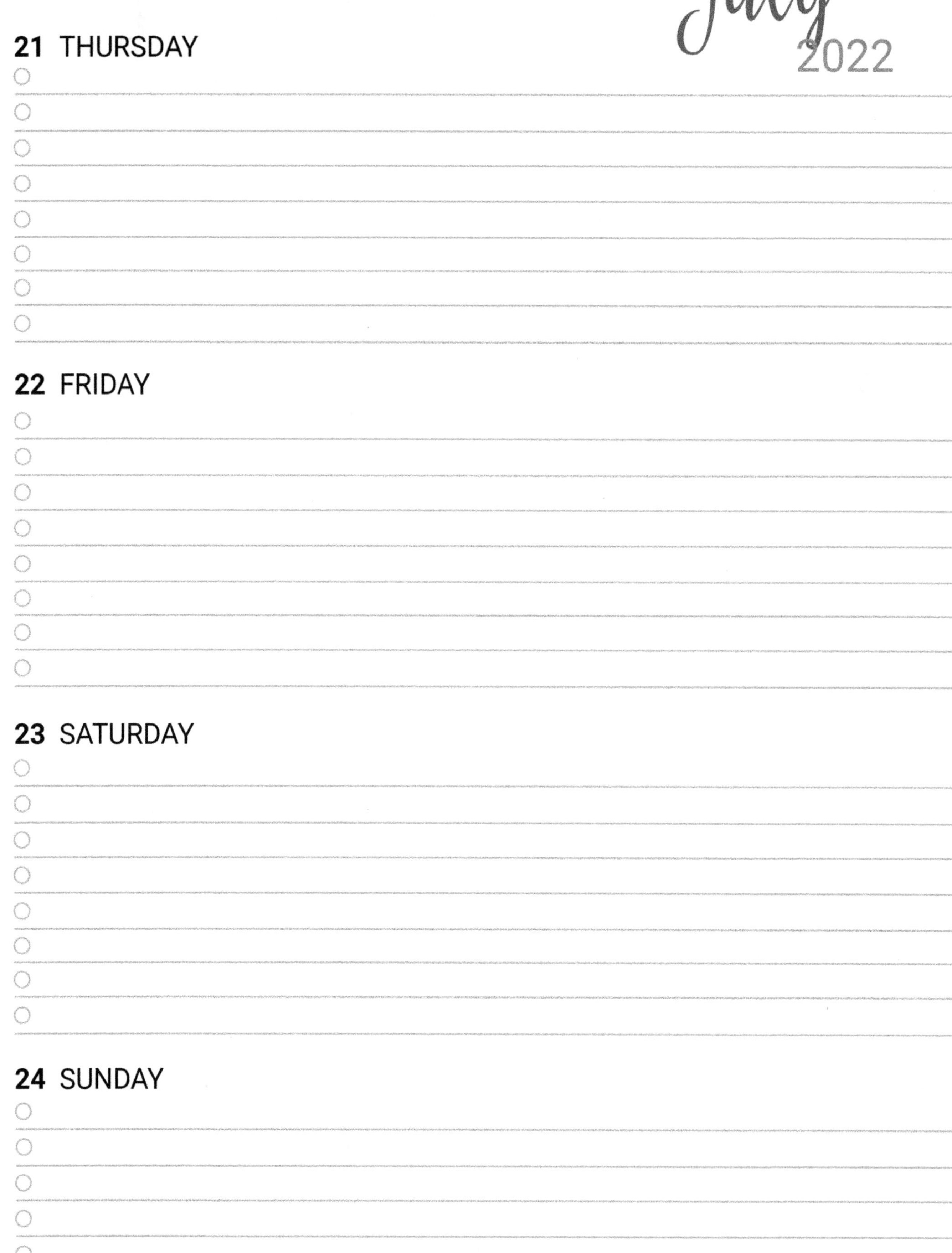

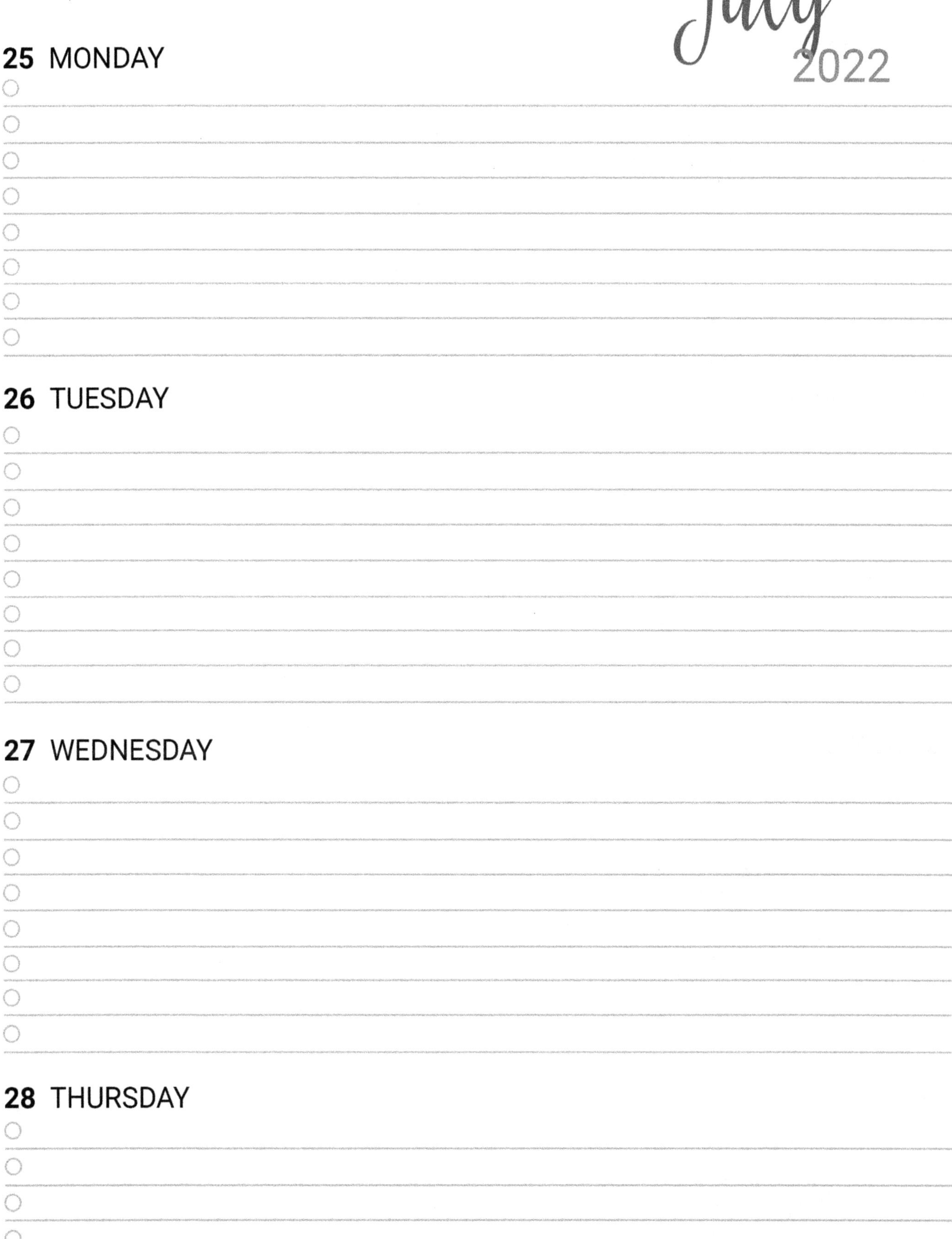

July
2022

25 MONDAY

26 TUESDAY

27 WEDNESDAY

28 THURSDAY

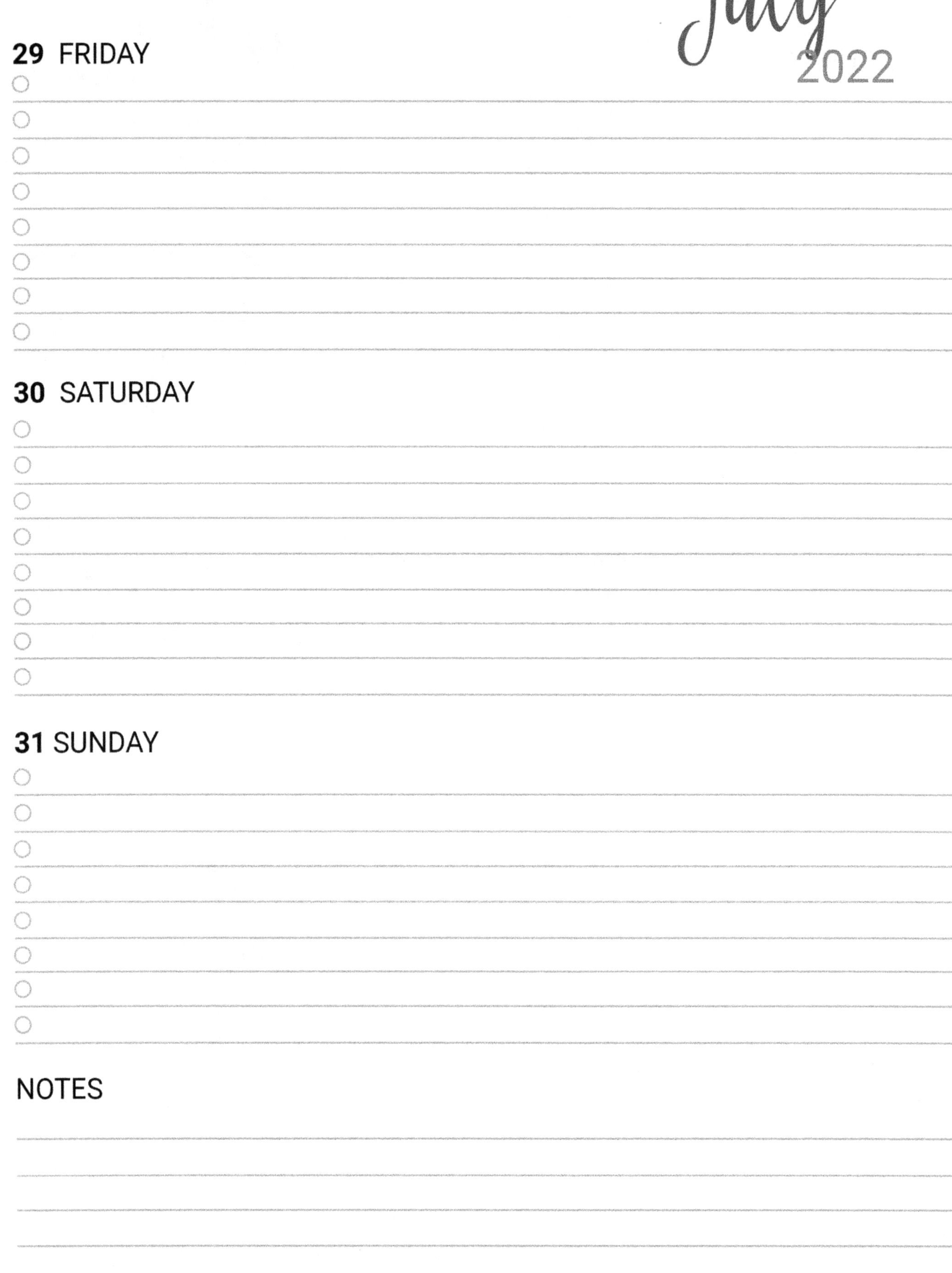

July
2022

29 FRIDAY

30 SATURDAY

31 SUNDAY

NOTES

01 MONDAY

○
○
○
○
○
○
○
○

02 TUESDAY

○
○
○
○
○
○
○
○

03 WEDNESDAY

○
○
○
○
○
○
○
○

04 THURSDAY

○
○
○
○
○

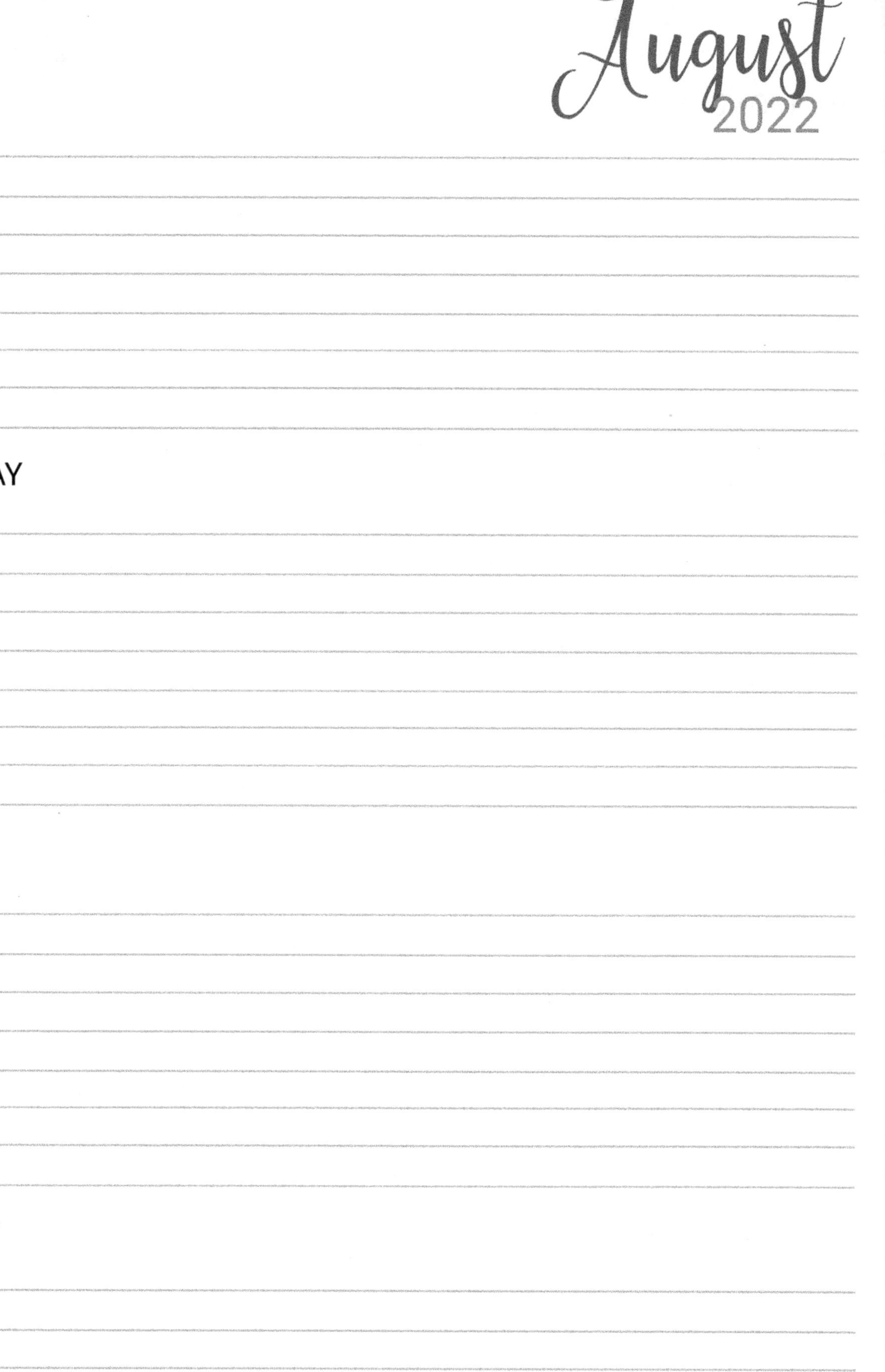

August
2022

05 FRIDAY

06 SATURDAY

07 SUNDAY

08 MONDAY

09 TUESDAY

10 WEDNESDAY

11 THURSDAY

12 FRIDAY

13 SATURDAY

14 SUNDAY

15 MONDAY

16 TUESDAY

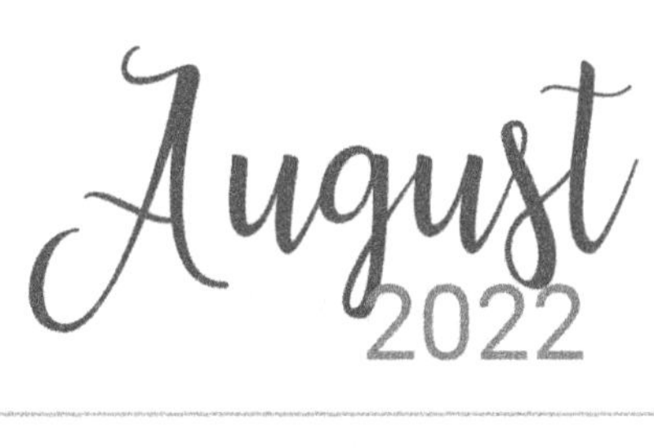

17 WEDNESDAY

18 THURSDAY

19 FRIDAY

20 SATURDAY

21 SUNDAY

22 MONDAY

23 TUESDAY

24 WEDNESDAY

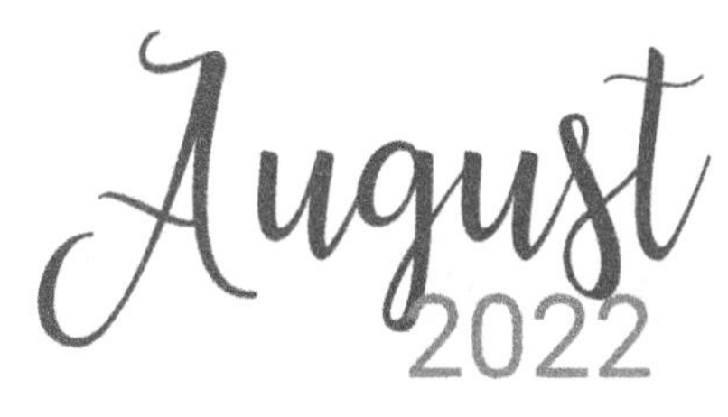

25 THURSDAY

26 FRIDAY

27 SATURDAY

28 SUNDAY

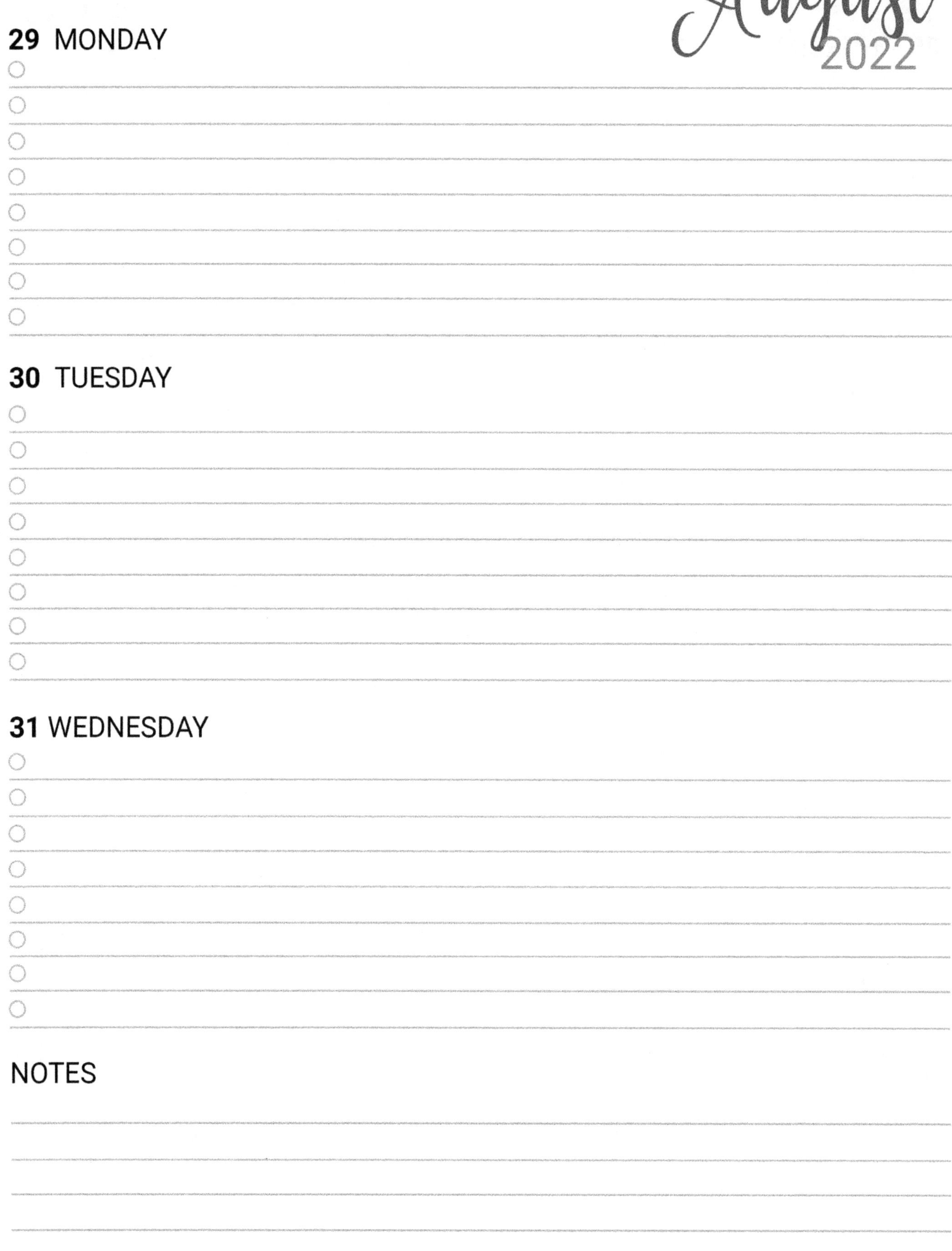

August
2022

29 MONDAY

30 TUESDAY

31 WEDNESDAY

NOTES

September
2022

01 THURSDAY

- ○
- ○
- ○
- ○
- ○
- ○
- ○
- ○

02 FRIDAY

- ○
- ○
- ○
- ○
- ○
- ○
- ○
- ○

03 SATURDAY

- ○
- ○
- ○
- ○
- ○
- ○
- ○
- ○

04 SUNDAY

- ○
- ○
- ○
- ○
- ○

05 MONDAY

○
○
○
○
○
○
○
○

06 TUESDAY

○
○
○
○
○
○
○
○

07 WEDNESDAY

○
○
○
○
○
○
○
○

08 THURSDAY

○
○
○
○
○

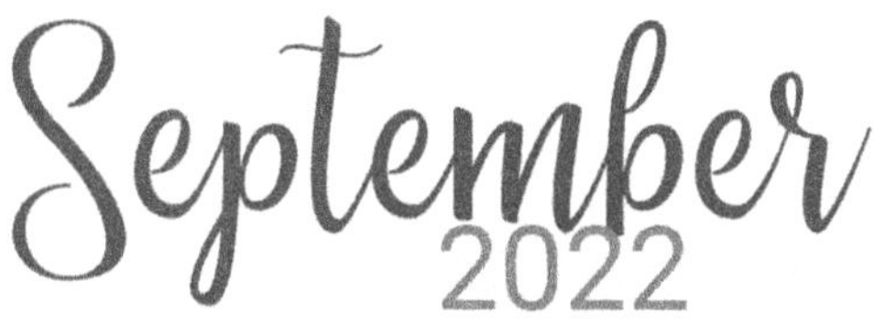

09 FRIDAY

10 SATURDAY

11 SUNDAY

12 MONDAY

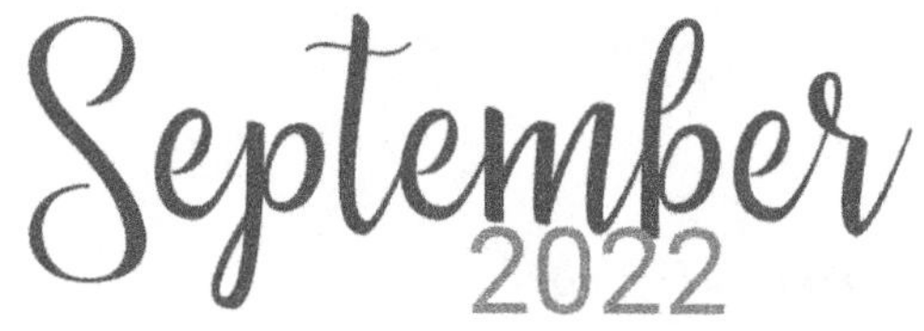

13 TUESDAY

14 WEDNESDAY

15 THURSDAY

16 FRIDAY

17 SATURDAY

18 SUNDAY

19 MONDAY

20 TUESDAY

21 WEDNESDAY

22 THURSDAY

23 FRIDAY

24 SATURDAY

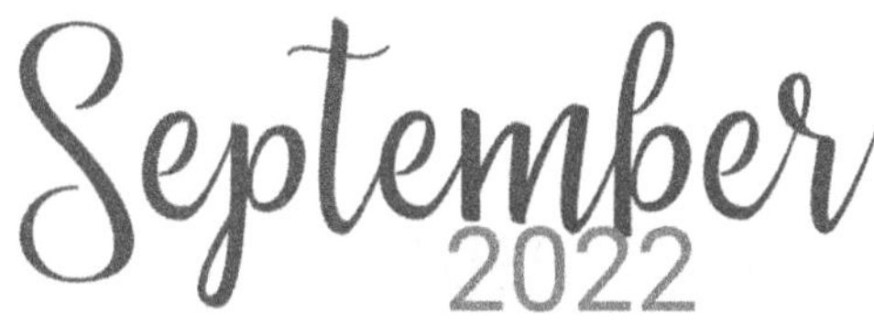

September
2022

25 SUNDAY

26 MONDAY

27 TUESDAY

28 WEDNESDAY

29 THURSDAY

-
-
-
-
-
-
-
-

30 FRIDAY

-
-
-
-
-
-
-
-

NOTES

October
2022

01 SATURDAY

02 SUNDAY

03 MONDAY

04 TUESDAY

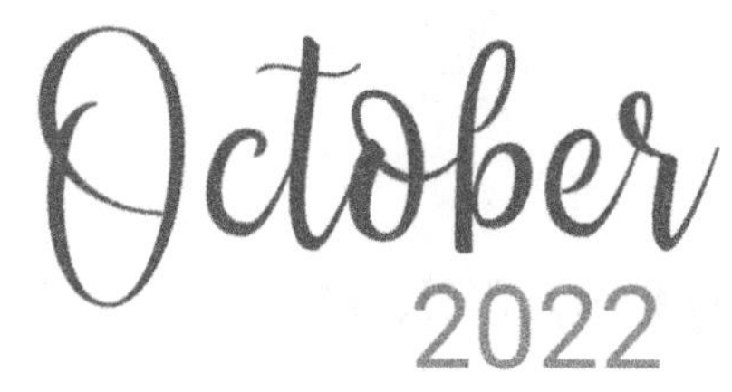

October
2022

05 WEDNESDAY

06 THURSDAY

07 FRIDAY

08 SATURDAY

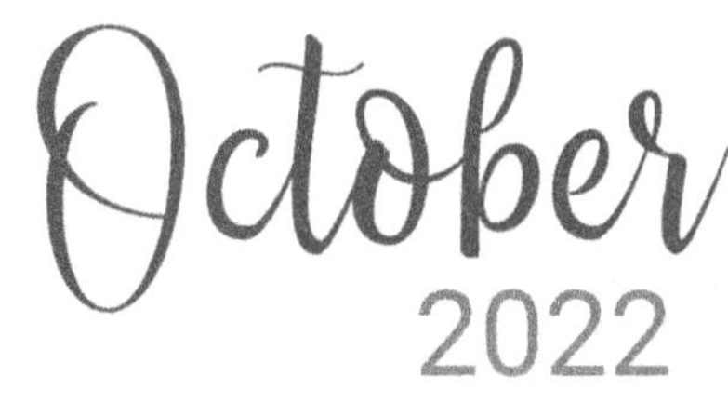

09 SUNDAY

10 MONDAY

11 TUESDAY

12 WEDNESDAY

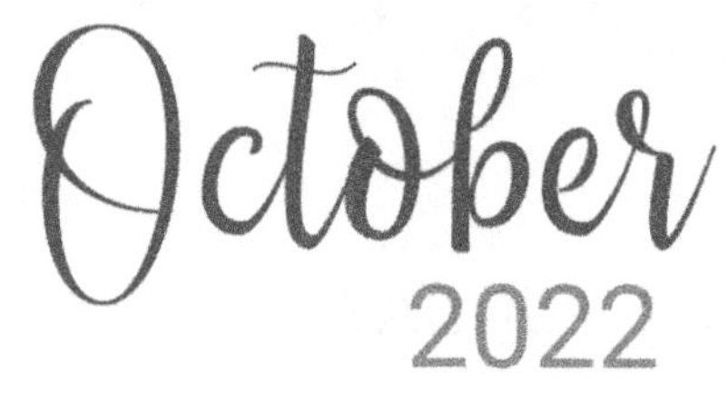

13 THURSDAY

14 FRIDAY

15 SATURDAY

16 SUNDAY

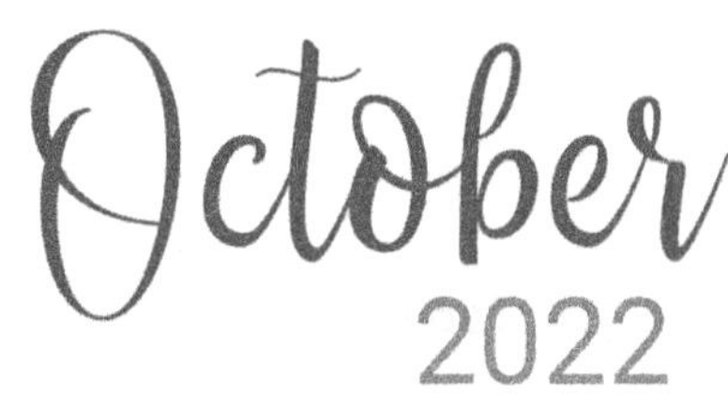

17 MONDAY

18 TUESDAY

19 WEDNESDAY

20 THURSDAY

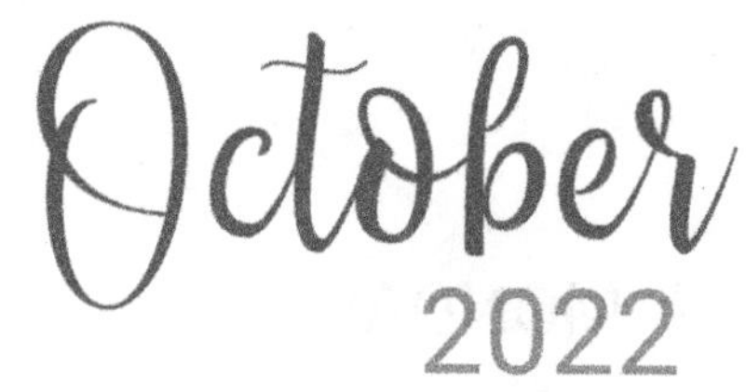

21 FRIDAY

22 SATURDAY

23 SUNDAY

24 MONDAY

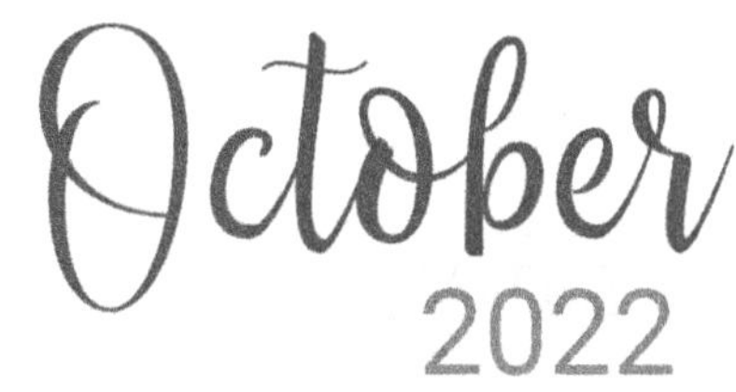

25 TUESDAY

26 WEDNESDAY

27 THURSDAY

28 FRIDAY

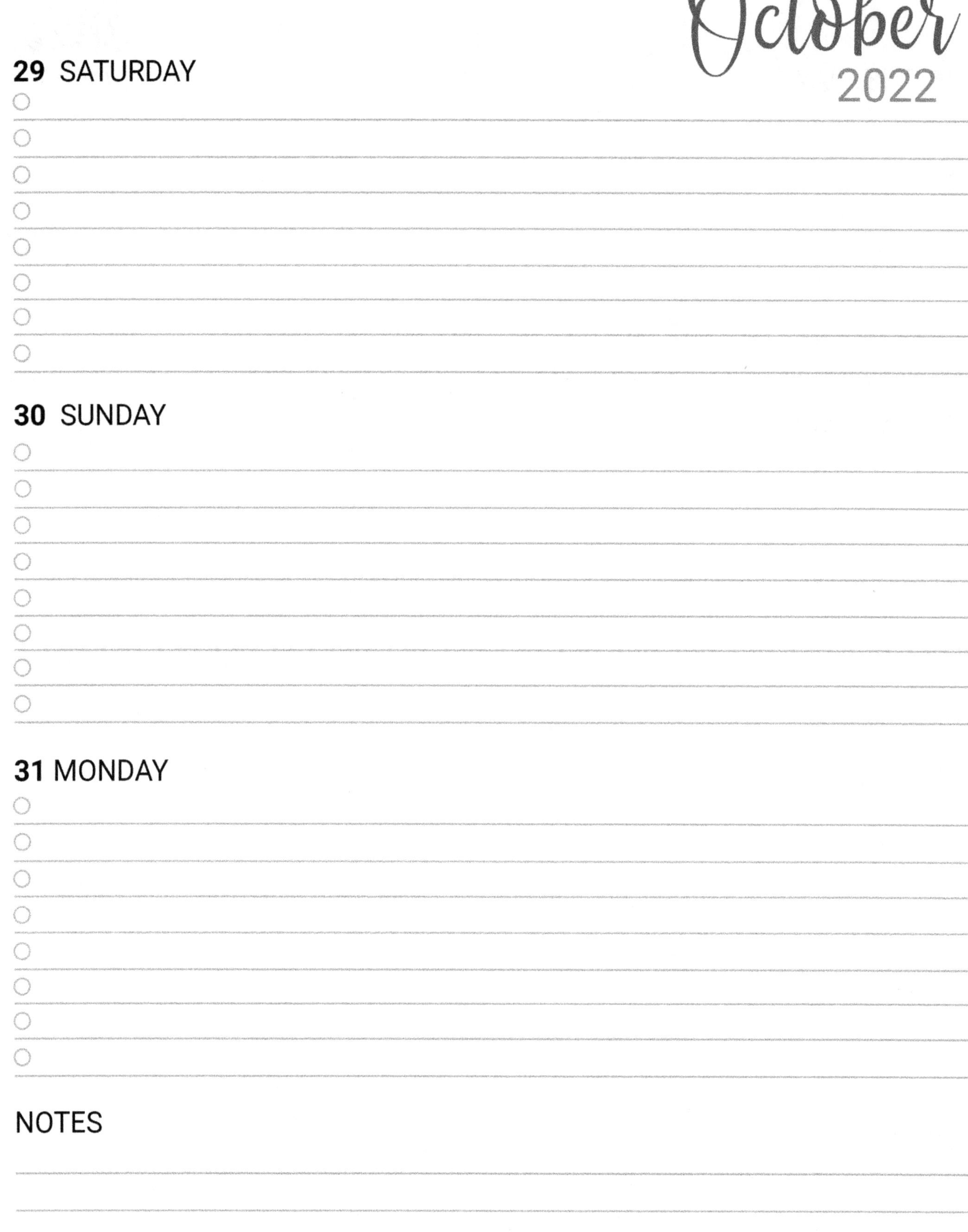

October
2022

29 SATURDAY

30 SUNDAY

31 MONDAY

NOTES

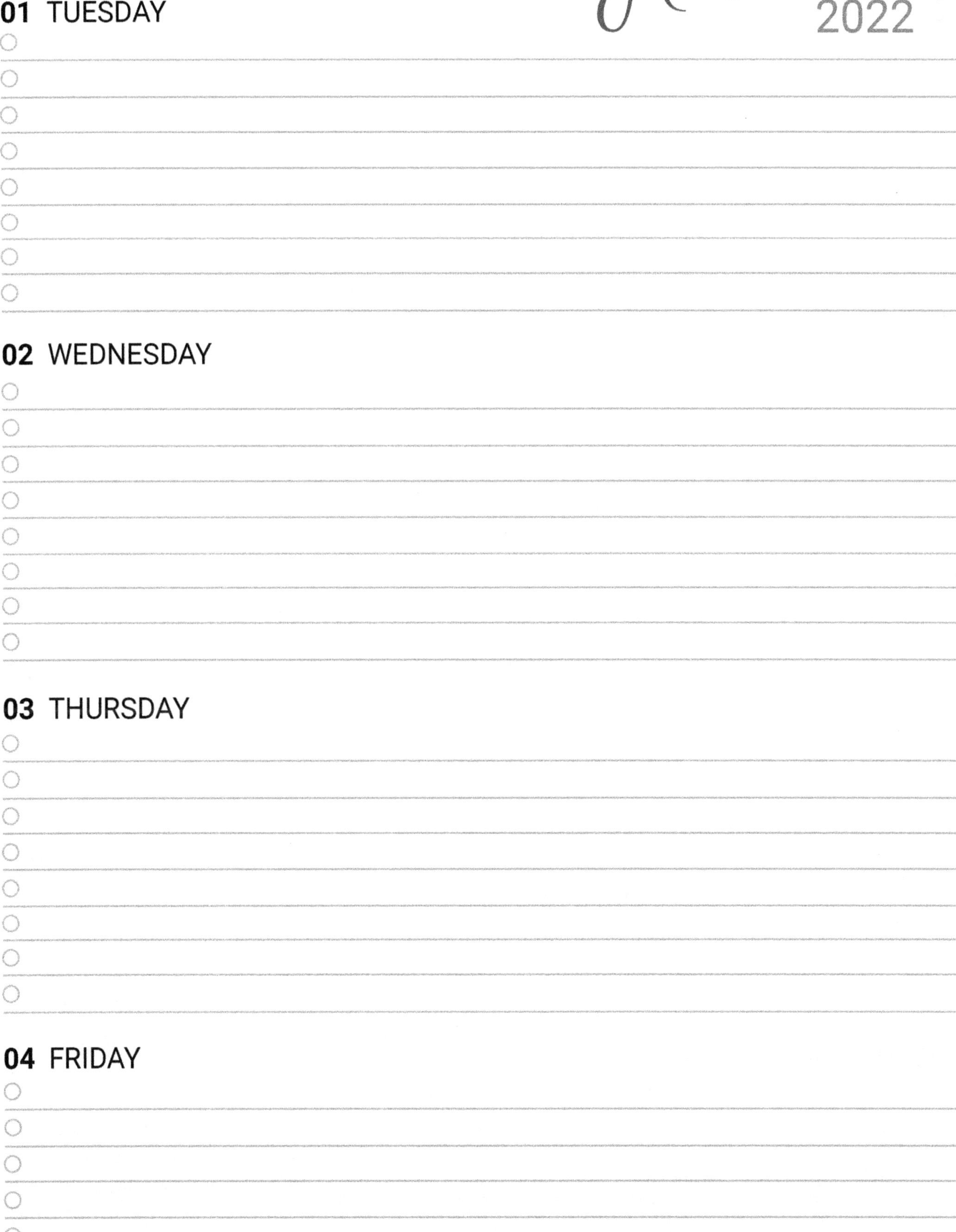

November
2022

01 TUESDAY

02 WEDNESDAY

03 THURSDAY

04 FRIDAY

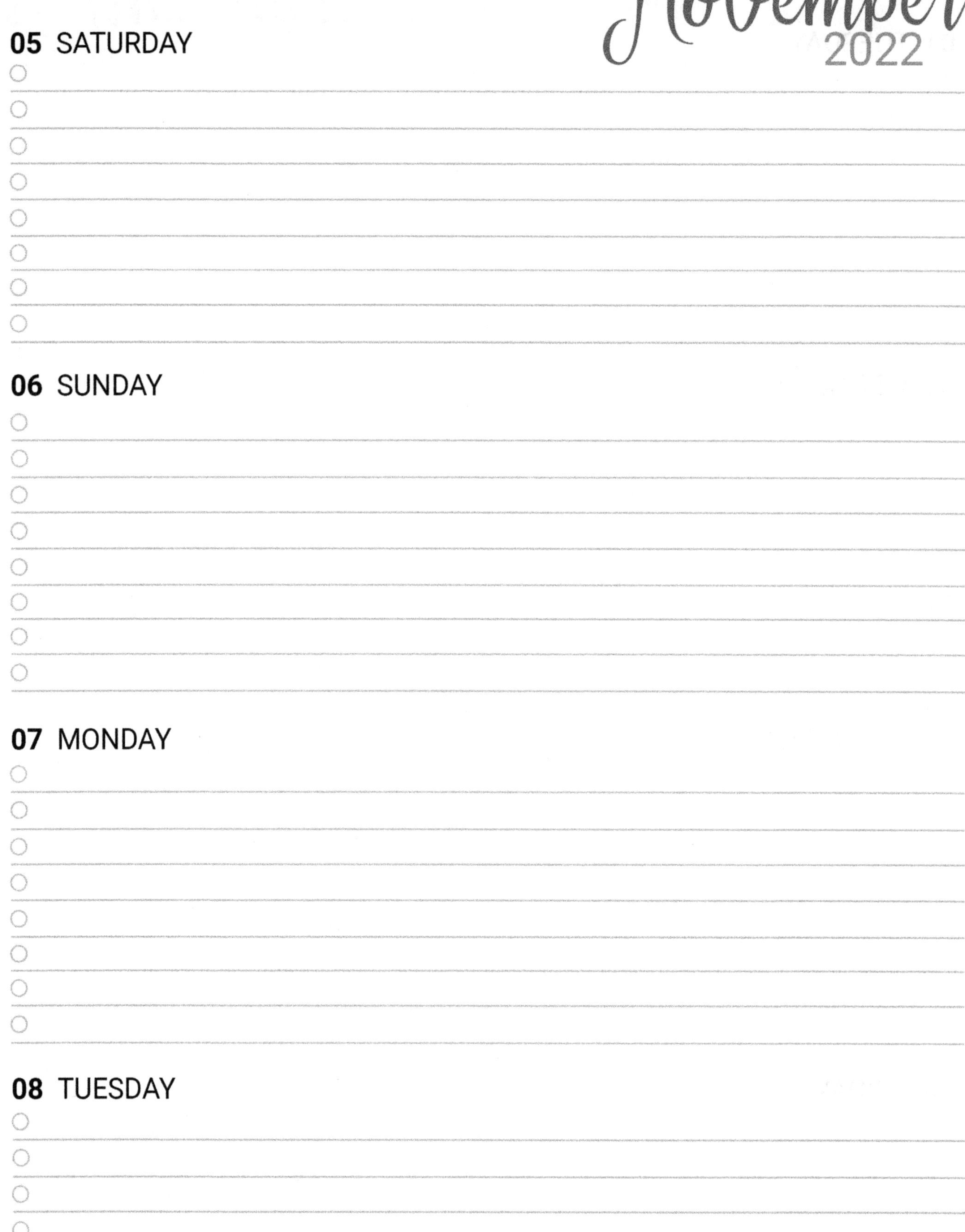

November
2022

05 SATURDAY

06 SUNDAY

07 MONDAY

08 TUESDAY

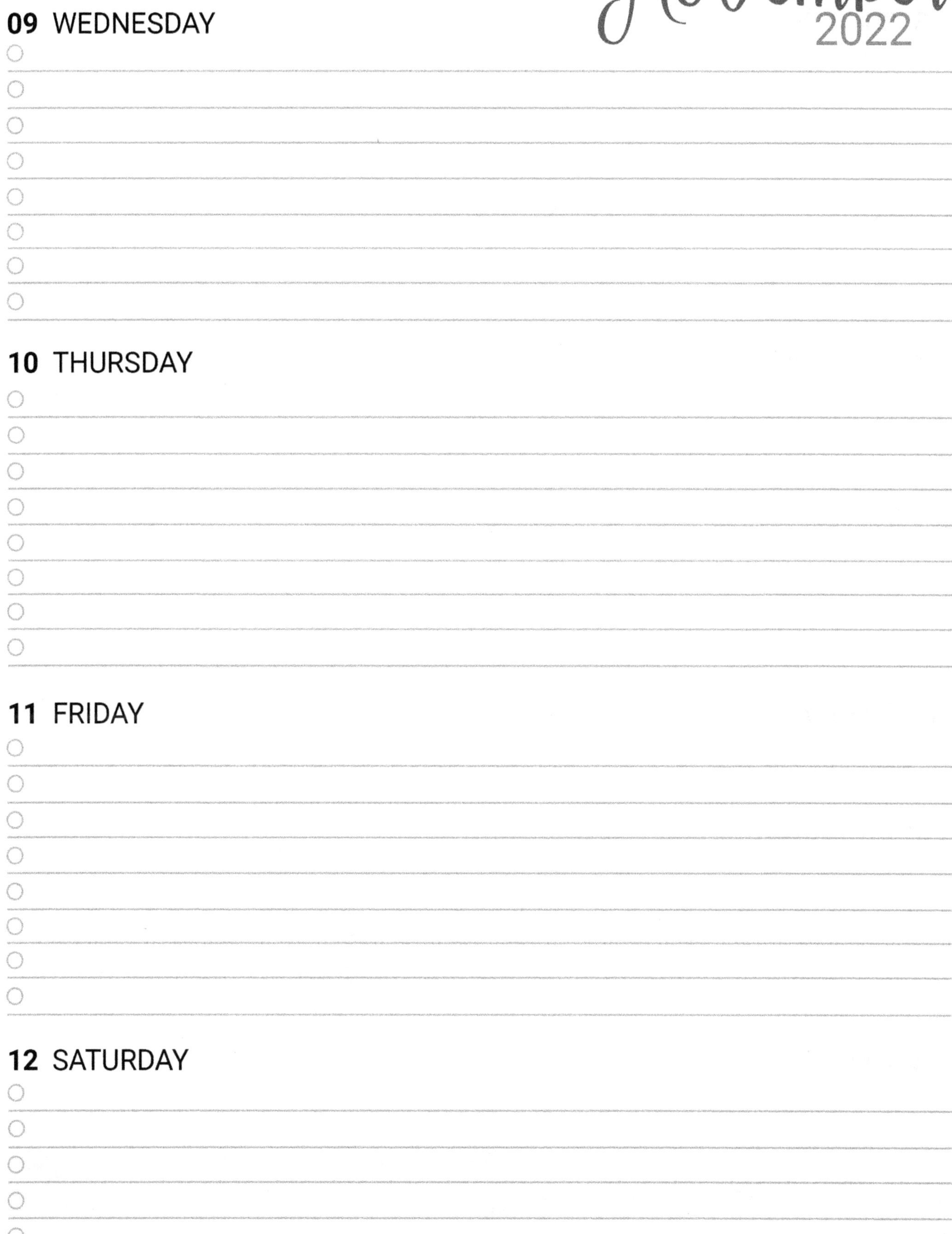

09 WEDNESDAY

10 THURSDAY

11 FRIDAY

12 SATURDAY

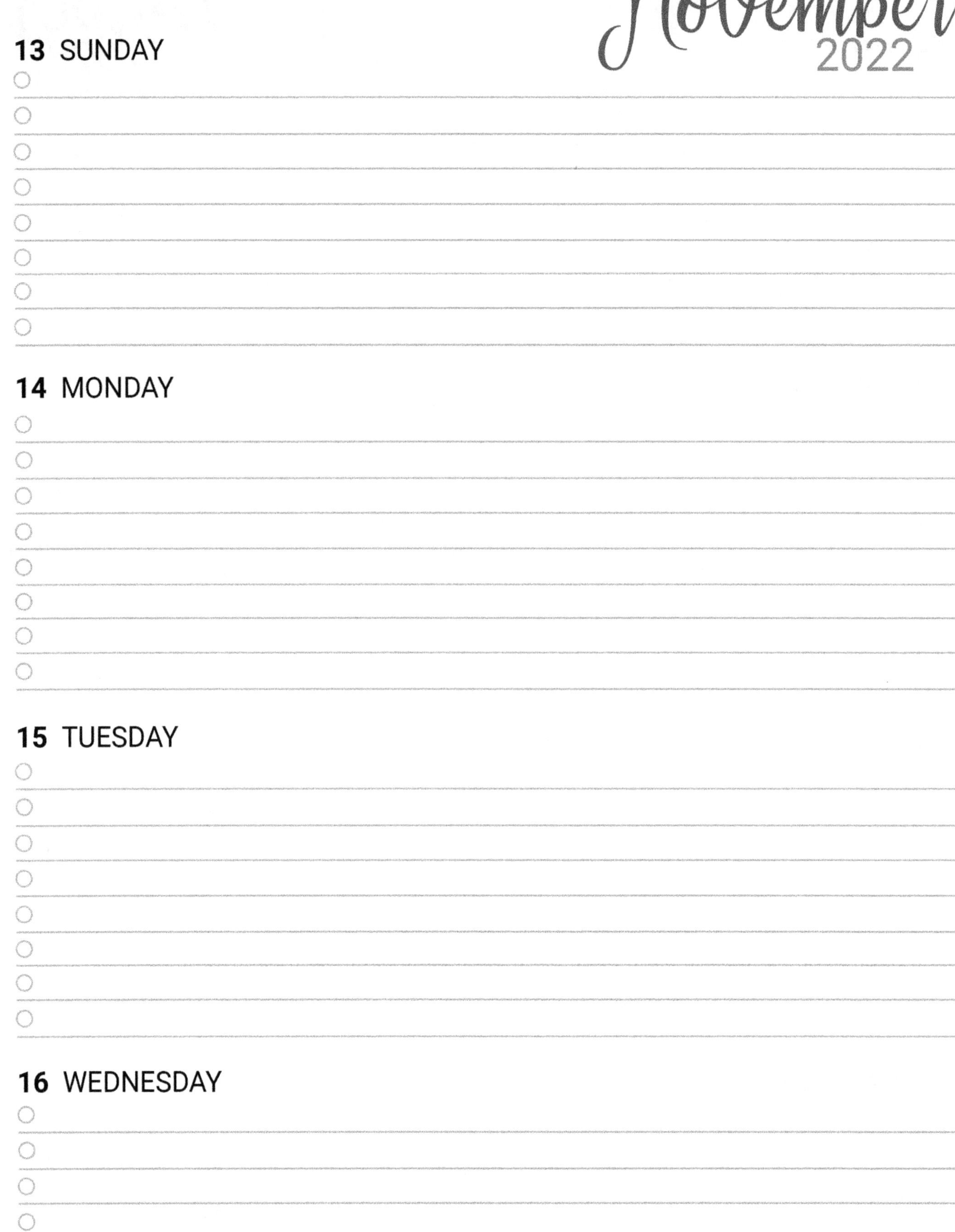

November
2022

13 SUNDAY

14 MONDAY

15 TUESDAY

16 WEDNESDAY

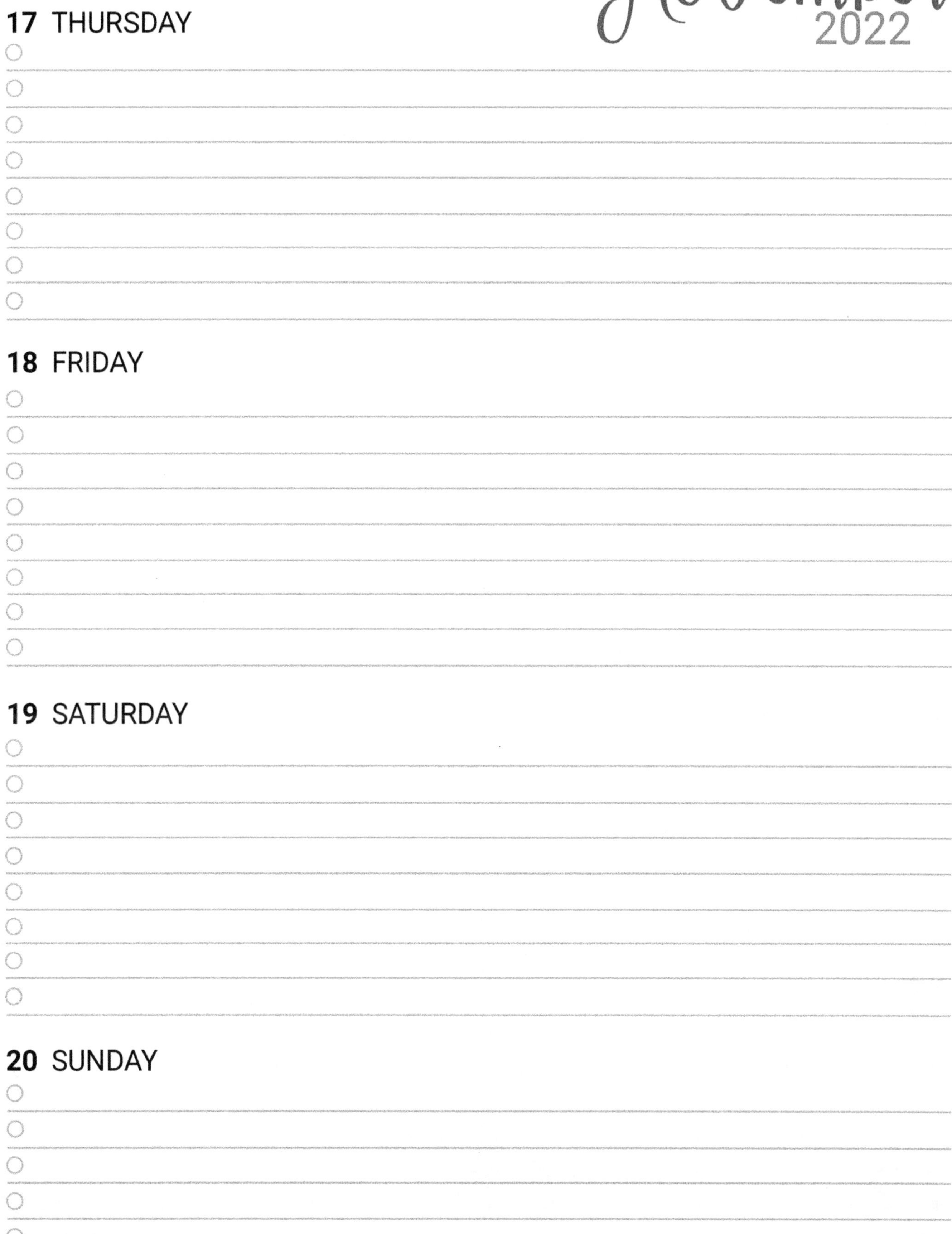

November
2022

17 THURSDAY

18 FRIDAY

19 SATURDAY

20 SUNDAY

21 MONDAY

22 TUESDAY

23 WEDNESDAY

24 THURSDAY

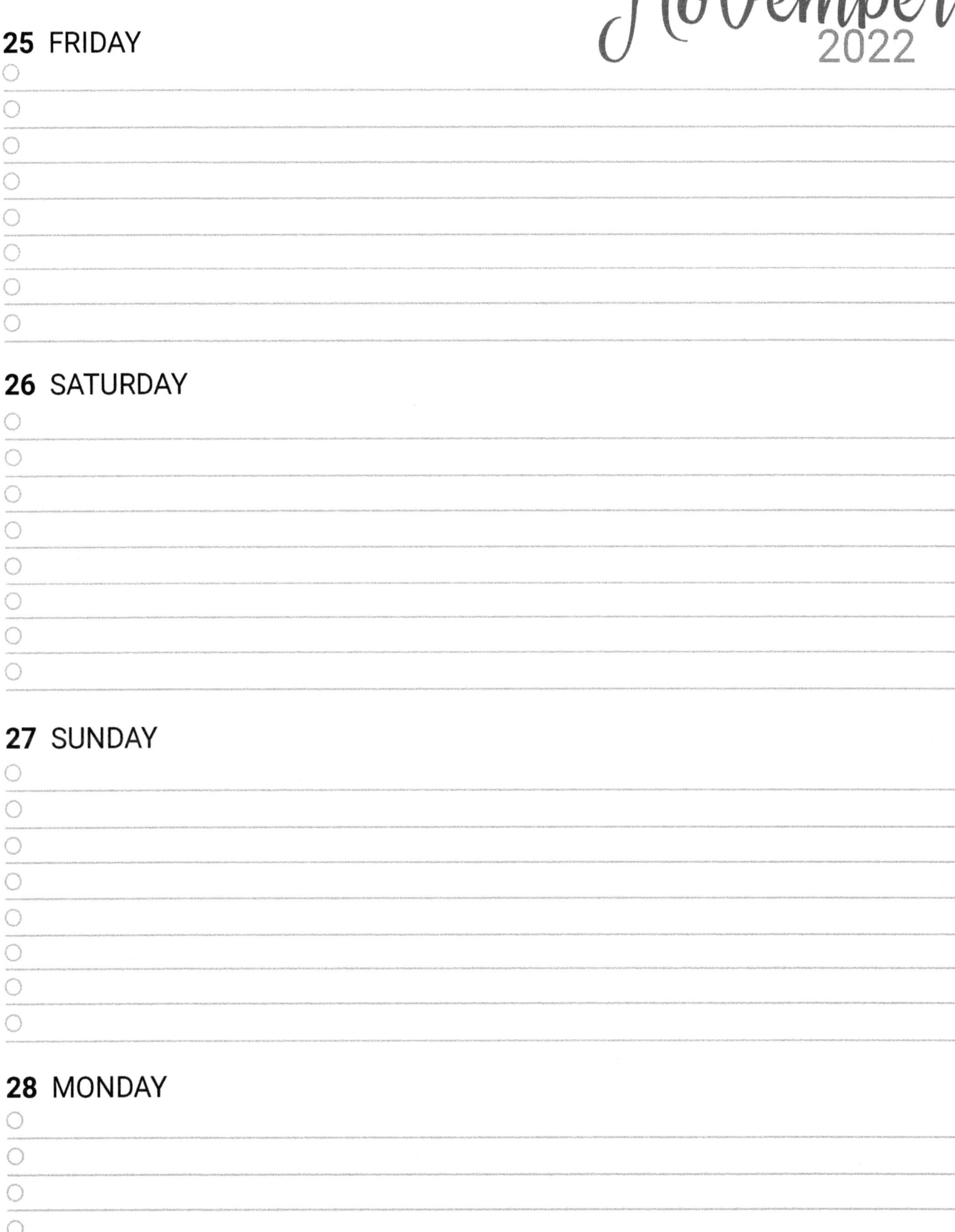

25 FRIDAY

26 SATURDAY

27 SUNDAY

28 MONDAY

29 TUESDAY

30 WEDNESDAY

NOTES

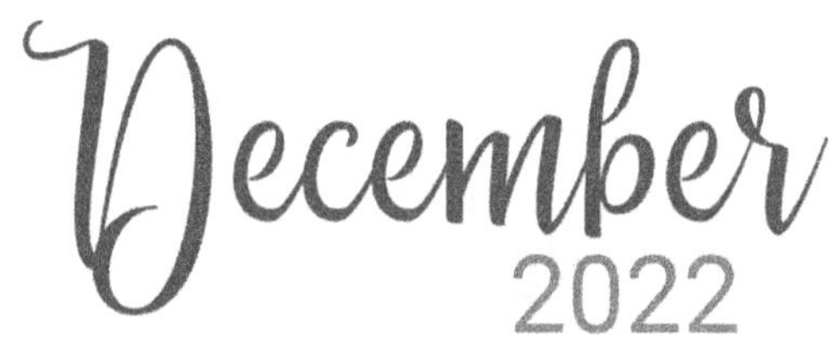

December
2022

01 THURSDAY

02 FRIDAY

03 SATURDAY

04 SUNDAY

05 MONDAY

06 TUESDAY

07 WEDNESDAY

08 THURSDAY

09 FRIDAY

10 SATURDAY

11 SUNDAY

12 MONDAY

13 TUESDAY

14 WEDNESDAY

15 THURSDAY

16 FRIDAY

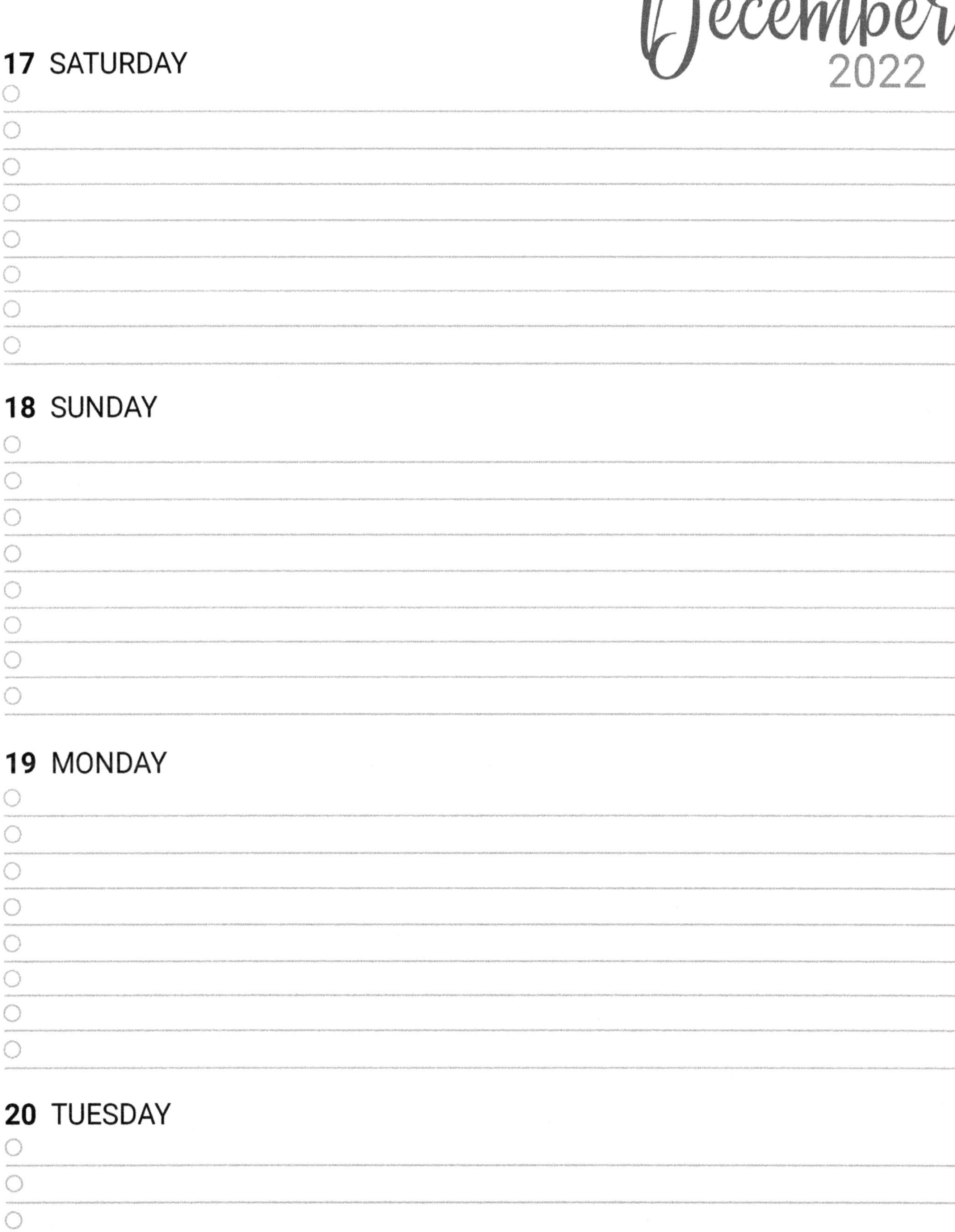

17 SATURDAY

18 SUNDAY

19 MONDAY

20 TUESDAY

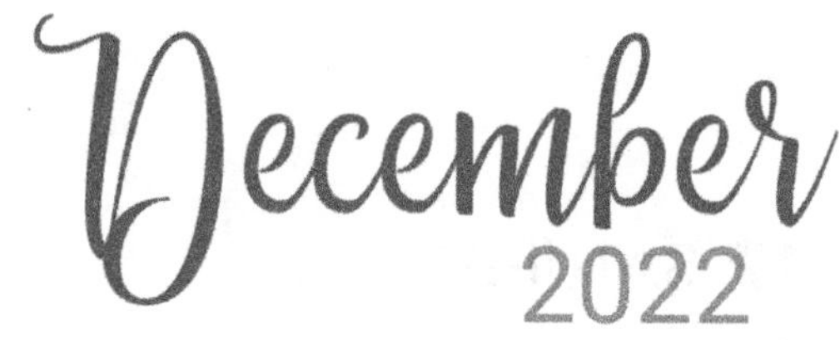

December 2022

21 WEDNESDAY

22 THURSDAY

23 FRIDAY

24 SATURDAY

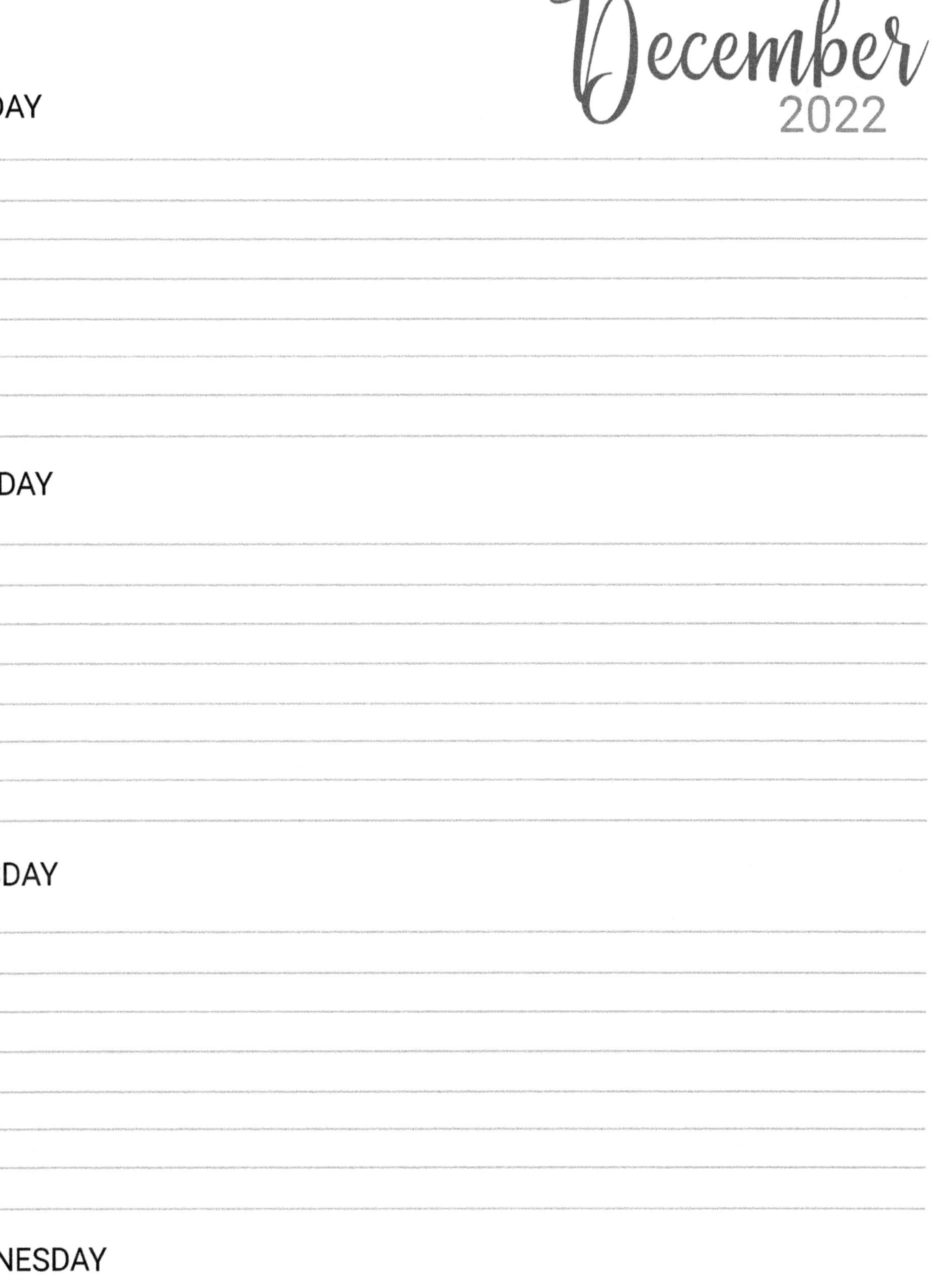

December
2022

25 SUNDAY

26 MONDAY

27 TUESDAY

28 WEDNESDAY

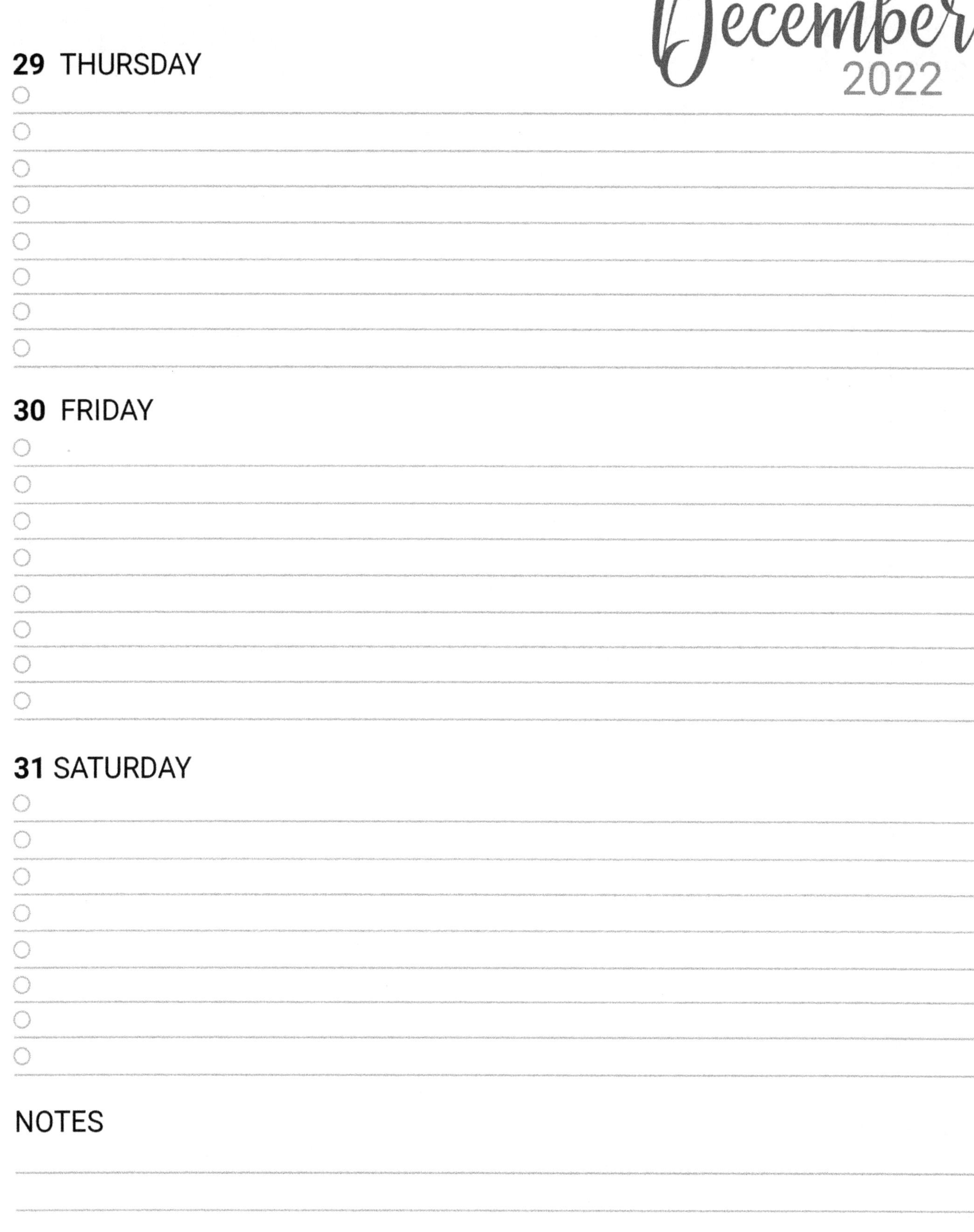

29 THURSDAY

30 FRIDAY

31 SATURDAY

NOTES